# Easy Grace

Meditations on Love, Awakening, & the Ecstatic Heart

## Also by David Spero

Beyond the place of laughter and tears
in the land of devotion
*Spiritual Writings of David Spero*

## David Spero Interviewed by David Rivers

The Dance of Stillness
*Exploring the Nature of Spiritual Awakening*
By David Rivers

# Easy Grace

Meditations on Love, Awakening,
& the Ecstatic Heart

## DAVID SPERO

DAVID SPERO
PUBLICATIONS

*Published and distributed in the United States by:*
David Spero Publications

www.DavidSpero.org
www.facebook.com/DavidSperoFriends

Excerpted talks edited by David Spero
Cover Photographs & Design by Daniele Weinberger

**Library of Congress Cataloging-in-Publication Data**

Spero, David.
    Easy Grace: Meditations on Love, Awakening and the
    Ecstatic Heart / David Spero.

    ISBN: 978-0-9701041-1-3
        1. Spirituality 2. Enlightenment 3. Metaphysical

Library of Congress Control Number: 2015918395

First Printing, May 2016

Printed in the United States of America

# Dedication

This book is dedicated to
my spiritual friends
all around the world.

May Non-Dual Silence,
Devotional Intoxication and Kundalini Shakti
wash through every being,
healing all forms of painful ignorance.

Let me be the seeds of your journey,

Let me be your wings of light.

[November, 2003]

# Contents

 part [1]

# 1  Meditation

part [4]

## 97 Devotion

## 🪷 part [5]

## 123 The Master

## part [6]

# 145 Realization

# Foreword

By Ramón Sender Barayón

In spiritual circles, the first question most frequently asked about a teacher is, "What is their lineage? Out of what tradition did they emerge? Who is their teacher and their teacher's teacher? Did they roam for years in the jungle subsisting on wild berries, or wall themselves up in a Himalayan cave?" Lineage somewhat parallels pedigrees in domesticated animals, and indeed the recitation of 'who begat whom' is deemed essential before a new teacher can take their place amongst the rows of credentialed gurus. As for jungle and cave experiences, these might be considered the equivalent of the 'curriculum vitae' within the professorial ranks.

What about David Spero? He comes to us with none of these. "No lineage? How presumptuous!" I can hear traditionalists mutter. I am reminded of the story of how the bumble bee should be incapable of flying because its body size relates poorly to its wingspread. Yet the bumble bee, unconcerned about aerodynamic theories, just goes ahead and flies anyway. In this case, the metaphor remains partially inaccurate because, in David Spero's case, he transmits nectar instead of collecting it. An Avatar does not require scientific proof, nor a stamped passport or visa.

The Divine Beloved once was described to me as recognizable in the physical manifestation by the following traits: Naked, Nameless, Homeless and Harmless. These traits also apply to the true Sanyasin in varying degrees, a personage with whom India is very familiar. However to these four, in David's case, we should also add the subtler energy qualities: Ineffable, Infinite, Fragrant and Free.

Just how do these eight characteristics apply? Beginning with 'Naked,' obviously David wears clothes when he moves about in the world but, on a more important level, he is 'shorn' of worldly adornments. He attaches no strings of initials after his name—Ph.D., LL.D, D.D., or any of those honorific bestowals with which the worldly distinguish themselves. He also presents himself completely as he is, and invites everyone else to do the same. Just come as you are. The Divine plays no favorites, although the more nakedly we approach Mother Kali through David, the more 'juicy a morsel' we tempt Her therewith. And reading David's life story, it becomes very obvious that Mother found him very tasty indeed! So we award David the 'N' for 'Naked.'

As for 'Nameless,' David has not assumed a religious name or title. He was born David Spero, and so he remains, auspiciously blessed from birth. His name itself contains many levels of meaning–"spero" means "hope" in Latin, and also evokes "breath" as in "aspire." Personally, I always have thought it best to retain one's given name and not assume a religious one that can exude an aroma of overblown sanctity–at least from the point of view of the secular western world. In India, where renaming upon ordination or surrender to the guru remains a hallowed tradition, the scent may retain its sweetness. Thus we add a second 'N.'

The third attribute, Homeless, implies that we are dealing with a wanderer. David indeed projects the quality of abiding nowhere, and yet his consciousness penetrates everywhere. Although based physically in California, he can project himself wherever he pleases. 'Homeless' also translates 'Sanyasin' into English, and defines living without attachment to all the accouterments that having a home implies. So we award an 'H.'

Harmless–Harmlessness or ahimsa, of course defines the trait hallowed by the nonviolent example of Gandhi-ji, but also includes the caring for and nurturing of all life forms. It implies a profound capacity to approach others with the same gentleness as a mother with her newborn. David's nonjudgmental tenderness towards others always evokes this quality of the Divine Mother. A second 'H.'

Ineffable–The next four traits take us above the four lower sheaths (physical, emotional, mental, astral), out of this manifesting world to levels unspeakably sacred and subtle where words begin to fail us. In the immaculate words of the Katha Upanishad, "How shall an ordinary person conceive THAT being for whom both priests and nobles are as food, and death a condiment?" David definitely is not ordinary in any sense of the word, so we award David an easy 'I' for ineffability.

Infinite–Once the lower sheaths are left behind, the soul-self travels freely throughout all realms of the cosmos. David has 'been there' and could have remained, but out of the infinite compassion that arises spontaneously in the heart of The Divine Beloved, he maintains his physical form to assist others' absorption into that vast Ocean of Self. A second 'I.'

Fragrant–Beyond the mundane exploitation of evocative aromas by the perfume industry exist the intoxicating scents of the Divine realms, attested to by various evolved souls. These subtle fragrances spontaneously arise in David's presence, and transmit truths that words otherwise fail to communicate. We attach an 'F.'

Free–In David Spero, we can welcome a living example of the Avatar, someone who has gone beyond all yogas and spiritual paths. He has merged with the Divine Mother Consciousness, the origin and resting place of all teachings and religions, and now returns to the lower dimensions at rest within the perfect freedom of amrita sahaja samadhi, the nectar-like natural state. In him we can identify what Sri Aurobindo referred to as a "forerunner of a divine multitude" and look ahead from his Living Transmission of the Divine to a time when, in the prophetic words of Swami Vivekananda, "Christs will be born like clusters of grapes."

I therefore commend all sincere aspirants to heed the precious words set down in the following pages by David Spero, The Divine Beloved, N.N.H.H.I.I.F.F.

# Preface

By Richard Schorske

*David: It's difficult for a human being to understand that the very reason for their birth is to awaken to what they already are. It's very insulting to the logical mind that devises plans of action, plans of what to become, that everything you are right now is actually sufficient to your existence. You don't need to attain anything.*

*I wonder if you can feel this Shakti, this Fire that's moving. It's from here to here (pointing heart to heart). It's not from here to here (pointing head to head). You know that it's really in the guts that I'm talking, not out of my head.*

*You're with me? Good.*

*Do you feel this Energy? Good.*

David Spero is an original. Born and raised in a working class neighborhood in Providence, Rhode Island, he awakened to his primordial nature at an extraordinarily young age; and in innocence, modesty, and near-secrecy, he has been teaching and transmitting the Love, Power, and Truth of the Heart ever since. Some years ago, I had the good fortune of being introduced to David by a long-time spiritual friend, Dr. Van Nguyen, who with a shy but sly grin, suggested I come for an evening sitting with David. When I entered the room with David, I was joined by perhaps two dozen other participants—as he likes to call his students, friends, and visitors alike. I had heard from Van and others that David transmitted a powerful yet sweet Heart-Energy, which David calls *Hridaya-Shakti* or Awakened Heart Consciousness. With only this modest introduction, I was not prepared for what I next experienced.

In the space of a short meditation and talk (in less than the time it takes to see a Hollywood movie), David was able to transmit this force of Heart Consciousness in a form so thick and tangible that I felt fully enveloped in a warm, blissful, Radiant Fog of Love, bringing all my cells to a feeling of extraordinary attention and fullness. Among our small group, he created a field of Consciousness, Energy, and Heart-Feeling so deep and wide that it defied any one explanation or expression. In dialogue after the meditation, some people described touching the Void, or the Absolute, while others described an intensification of Consciousness and Love at the heart, and virtually all of us felt a powerful tingling and Enlivening Energy permeating the air like a steam bath, entering and cleansing the pores of the body and the soul. For myself, I felt an instant recognition of spiritual mastery—yet in the most intimate form—as if in re-union with a dear friend or family member. I felt loved and almost supernaturally known, from head to toe, yet also invited into a highly personal and ordinary-human directness of relationship.

I left that first meeting with a strong desire to deepen my acquaintance with David's Spiritual Energy and wisdom.

Through online webcasts offering meditation and dialogue, abundant videos, and his magnificent short volume of talks and writings—*Beyond the Place of Laughter and Tears in the Land of Devotion*—I came to a clear realization. David was demonstrating a new approach to spiritual reality, one that I have come to know as Easy Grace.

What is Easy Grace? In contrast to the countless ways of religious ritual, dogmatic belief, or endless self-development, David's Easy Grace offers a most simple and direct opportunity to awaken and abide in the Bliss of Consciousness Itself. Not through self-effort, but through reception (by Grace) of the unconditional love and trust so magnanimously present in David's company.

When I first felt the power of this Heart-Transmission, I confess to being a little fearful. Having witnessed the exploits of patriarchal gurus and hierarchical religions, I was concerned that if I fully allowed this powerful force to enter me, would there be a "bait and switch" coming later? Would my cherished autonomy or freedom be compromised? Over a period of time, I determined *not* to surrender more deeply until I looked at David from all sides. I wanted to feel sure he was not lusting for power, or hiding any ethical skeletons. Considering that David has spent nearly two decades teaching in public, I was happily surprised to find in his community an extremely modest and small gathering, essentially devoid of politics or institutional form, and (for the first time in my experience of spiritual community) I could find no heavy shadows of money, sex, politics, and power. That in itself seemed a not-so-minor miracle. And yet I discovered that this benign scene also fits David's character, as I progressively discovered in him an uncompromised devotion to Freedom in all beings and things.

Reassured of David's integrity and trustworthiness at the outer level, I began sinking deeper into an inner mystery. I began to feel that my lifelong and relentless urge toward seeking for some kind of liberation was coming to an end. Through David's Spiritual Transmission, I felt that my meditation (and all other forms of psycho-spiritual effort) was becoming David's own "spiritual business" and that I could relinquish my adventure of striving toward some kind of inner quiet or transcendental breakthrough. Paradoxically, as I listened to David's words, I felt that his Blessing was taking form as Energy—as a misted, graceful, Atomic Force with its own momentum and destiny. I could cooperate with this Energy and Being through love, surrender, and trust, such that no kind of self-effort or subservience would be required of me.

It was then that strange miracles began to unfold. Or maybe they had already begun in the two or three months before I met David. Just prior to that first meeting, seemingly out of nowhere, I began to have a very strange upwelling of awareness and devotional feeling toward Krishna, the legendary Hindu deity who is variously depicted as a child, a lover, a sage, and even a great Avatar (an Incarnation of the Divine.) While I had no special knowledge or affinity for Krishna, I found myself listening continuously to Krishna-themed chants, and becoming curious about Krishna's nature, as if he was coming to join my spiritual family. When I then met David in the flesh, I was shocked by a familiar correspondence to qualities which had already become intimate to me. David-as-Krishna (or Krishna-as-David) felt enormously playful, humorous, obviously free, occasionally fierce, emanating intense light, poetic and vulnerable, radiating profoundly personal yet Transcendent and Unconditional Love. And doing all this simultaneously with an entire room full of spiritual friends.

Some weeks after my initial encounter with David, I was in the bathroom innocently getting ready for bed when a bolt of Energy shot through me out of nowhere. I fell on the floor laughing out loud as my mind was overwhelmed with the recognition that whoever David is, he is now appearing in a modern version of this ancient and eternal "avataric" archetype. The intuition flashed that he is here to grant Spiritual Blessing and Awakening through *profoundly Easy* Grace as a boon, or a free gift—not as a reward for being a bit less naughty or a lot more nice. I was overcome with laughter and Heart-Joy at the simplicity and power of David's Grace, and I shouted over and over "it's you, it's you, it's You!"

One might suppose by this point that an earnest aspirant might have taken up a life of fullest trust and devotion. I'm embarrassed to say—still not yet! In the following months, I determined to test David's efficacy as a Spiritual Force by setting up deliberate tests, a highly adolescent approach which I do not recommend! One day I prayed for the instant appearance of financial resources that had been held up by bureaucratic processes, and asked for a sign to be given within twenty minutes. When I returned from a walk on the beach to my car and cell phone, three communications from three different sources had arrived that money was on the way—one with the e-mail heading, "it's a miracle." Another day, I prayed for the appearance of a loving partner in 90 days, and that was granted, at almost exactly the 90-day mark. I prayed for the spiritual and physical well-being of my son (to help move beyond an addiction) and my father (to release a fear of death), and these remarkable outcomes manifested in a most compelling way. I could go on—from the minor to the major keys of life. Is this everyone's experience of David? I presume not—or at least not immediately. Yet I have heard so many others testify to extraordinary graces of like magnitude.

Miracles aside, David is so exceedingly modest. His power to grant "boons," or respond to heart-felt prayers, was only very reluctantly revealed to him through his relationship with the Divine Mother (described in depth in an interview in David Rivers' book, *The Dance of Stillness*). Through the most intense years of David's own practice and awakening, the Divine Mother somehow merged with David's own Being in a kind of spiritual supernova: a unique union of Divine-Feminine and Divine-Masculine, creating in turn a new and unique potency of Radiant Blessing in the manifest realms.

In addition to (or as another form of) his Energetic Blessings and miracles, there is this dimension of David's Easy Grace: his highly poetic teaching style. David meets his friends and participants in formal public settings, but he never comes with a prepared speech or homily. In spontaneous dialogue with students, David offers pearls of wisdom that empha-size direct and immediate reception of the Awakened Heart Consciousness so tangible in his company. This Vibratory Transmission paradoxically is felt to emanate from David, yet it also feels all-pervasive and in-dwelling in every individual.

Even as he provides access to this Sublime Energy, David also fields the inevitable questions of aspirants about psycho-spiritual "problems" and "stuff." In response to the usual challenges and concerns about conditional existence, David compassionately redirects attention to the speaker's own native intelligence—noting specific evidence that the student has *already* begun to witness, understand, and move beyond problematizing consciousness. And he points to the reality that the indwelling and inherent joy is *always* present, even as the inevitable pain of the human condition continues to rise and fall.

After experiencing the balm of David's spoken teaching for a year or more, it occurred to me that a new volume of talk excerpts would be a great blessing to his students and the general public alike. When I asked David if I might edit such a volume for him, he graciously gave permission to roam freely among his transcribed talks and bring together some of the most felicitous expressions of his genius. In my view, David's words have a unique place among the greatest literature of spirituality—for they combine a disarming simplicity of form with a profoundly liberating message of pure reliance on Grace, and the always-present Hridaya-Shakti, so freely granted in David's spiritual company.

Whether one is more attracted to the spiritual methods of insight, or meditation, or devotion, David's words bring a freshness, an innocence, and a mysterious power of Awakened Heart Consciousness to the subject at hand. Moreover, these brief passages and aphorisms contain a poetic resonance that, when experienced even in brief encounters at night or through the day, establish a kind of morphic field in which miracles may abide. *Easy Grace*, indeed.

*San Rafael, California | October 2015*

*Richard Schorske has been a spiritual friend of David Spero since 2012. He practiced Transcendental Meditation and belonged to the spiritual community of the late Adi Da Samraj. He has been a civic entrepreneur in the fields of education, clean energy, and climate action, and is currently founder/Executive Director of the Zero Net Energy Alliance. He has two grown children and lives with his partner in Marin County, California.*

# Acknowledgements

This book could not have been completed without the generous support I received from many people. I would like to especially thank the many transcribers who have worked quietly behind the scenes. Without their dedicated service, this book could not have come to completion.

**Transcriptions:** Abha Ohri & her team
**Editors:** Richard Schorske, Orley Lilly & Vivian Andrews
**Proofreading:** Kanthi Datla, Marcella Contento & Mark Andrews
**Webmaster:** Paul Brelin

## Art & Photo Credits by Page

Mark Andrews • 95
Sherry Burkhart • 93, 96
Josie Keys • xxx
Orley Lilly • 222
Caryn Oresky (Samadhi) • vi, xxviii
Antara Scales • 94
David Spero • 21, 24, 98, 188, 207, 210
Jeff Symonds • xxxv, 2
James Toole • 185
Daniele Weinberger • xxix, 124

# Special Acknowledgment

Orley Lilly's hard work, brilliance and charm
fill everyone's lives with Grace.

[2005]

# Introduction

This book is offered as an extended arm of my Grace-Filled Spiritual Transmission, composed of Non-Dual Light, Devotional Intoxication, Kundalini-Shakti, and Multi-dimensional Colors in Consciousness.

Non-Dual Light creates subjective effects in consciousness such as mental quietude, emotional tranquility, sensations of release and liberation, apprehension of no-self, plunging into pre-cognitive or non-cognitive silence, realization of emptiness and witnessing, along with other forms of temporary absorptions in the Absolute. In its highest phase, it describes Self-Realization, a state in which the Light of Being is fully established in human awareness.

Devotional Intoxication (whose essence is Divine Love) manifests as Unrestricted Feeling unleashed by the power of Pure Being. Appreciation, reverence, surrender, gratitude, compassion, longing, sublimity, worshipfulness, and seeing the most exquisite forms of beauty—these are some symptoms of the presence of Divine Love. In its highest manifestation, it is Absolute Being worshipping Itself as Total Feeling.

Kundalini-Shakti is the Energetic Arm of Non-Dual Light.

Its essential qualities are Intensity, Moving Current(s) and Vibrational Fullness, coursing through the human body. Subjective experience of Kundalini-Shakti corresponds with full animation of the body-mind, from head to toe, in Bio-Energetic Force, which may go on to acquire union with the Self. In raising human frequency sufficiently, to the threshold of the Absolute's Location, Kundalini-Shakti thus becomes an Energetic Ladder into Infinite Being. When stable, it becomes a constant expression of Absolute Being.

Of the Multi-Dimensional Colors in Consciousness, we can say they insinuate themselves gently during meditation into awareness, arising mainly in the forehead area as circles, dots, waves, undulating patterns: reds and blues, pinks, purples and gold, magenta, white, shades of green, all depicting worlds within worlds—what in Vedic lore are called lokas. They heal and balance the human nervous system in its ascension toward Divine Realization.

In addition to these Four Cosmic Transmissions, and as a result of experiencing them, there is also the creation of Soma, Soma Juice, or Amrita (also referred to as Amrita Nadi) throughout the body, which allows for steady and ongoing tasting of the Bliss of the Self.

Innocence is the Foundational Reality and Passive Principle organizing (and directing) these Four Arms of the Absolute. In time, these Four Arms culture and transform a human being's existence to luminous and ongoing recognition of Infinite Bliss.

These Four Transmissions, though empirically and linguistically distinct, arise united, and together comprise various flavors within One Absolute Being. Through them a deep impact ensues upon human attention and its knowing processes. Quickly, they elevate human attention into the Divine Condition.

Thus, as fluctuations of one Ultimate Reality, Non-Dual Light, Devotional Intoxication, Kundalini-Shakti, and Multidimensional Colors activate specific forms or avenues of human awakening as well as cause to blossom those ontological and epistemological structures necessary for the complete transformation of the human being.

The Self, remaining free from penetrative analyses born of thought and language, shines in all directions and to all beings. Living in its Perfect Aloneness, it stays unalloyed in the hearts of all. It becomes "known" by the activities of inductive and deductive reasoning, simultaneously informed by the great revelations arising from yogic, meditative and mystical experience.

Discrimination between the Absolute and relative occurs spontaneously through the reception of Spiritual Grace and Activated Divine Transmission. Ongoing revelations of the Self's Qualities allow the finite mind to conclude, with clarity, humility and confidence: "I am That, Thou art That, That alone is."

Finally, it is prudent to consider the Self or Absolute Being to be nothing less than the default setting of mind itself, beyond the fields of opposites rather than a summoned or attained experience, or even a "superior" reality created specifically for human beings. For paradoxically the Self stays free even of Its own realizations.

Divine Self-Recognition is shared in this book of quotations from beginning to end.

May you taste and enjoy its Liberating Grace.

David Spero
October 6, 2014

Real meditation is an act of negation. The effect, the profound consequence of true meditation, is a tremendous act of negation. It's a funneling, a pooling, of all the energies and capacities of the human being, drawing them into a singular mode of perception.

part [1]

# Meditation

[2012]

# Meditation, Sublimity, and Grace

The mood of meditation is the mood of sublimity itself.

This sublime feeling can be described as the inner being falling into itself, the inner being bowing down to itself, surrendering into itself, so that for a short moment, there is no other, no sense of otherness, no object-based perception.

This is what I mean by sublime: to be released of oneself, to transcend oneself easily, without friction, without effort, without fear.

It's a joy to feel one's life merge into That which is beyond it. This is a gift, a Divine Gift.

*The Ocean of Liberated Bliss, April 16, 2002, DVD #59*

# In Meditation, One Really Does Become Like a Child before That Vastness

Meditation is a great mystery. It is a profound and unfathomable topic. The subject of meditation is the nature of the self. The object of meditation is also the nature of the self and it is also that which unites the subject and the object.

At some blessed point, meditation is no longer practiced but is a full, palpable realization. Meditation does not function while the intellect is scrutinizing. The intellect enters into a spontaneous state of self-surrender. In that state of self-surrender, the Full Reality then can give birth to itself without disturbance.

So, one really does become like a child before that vastness.

Once meditation is truly triggered, it keeps on happening spontaneously, over and over again, until this self-culmination of profound awakeness occurs.

This is really an ecstatic topic, how one comes to be able to live so close to the edge of one's life that even living day by day is like a near-death experience. One has become so thin, so translucent, and so vulnerable that the reality, the Cosmic Reality, can unveil itself through your awakened life. It is an excruciating state to live in. One is no longer kept safe and protected.

*The Essence of the Real, May 7, 2002, DVD #W-2*

# To Be Thrust from the Conceptual into the Real Is the Essence of the Awakened Life

Right in this moment, this spacious moment, this innocent moment, this non-moment, one can feel that something is arising as Consciousness, not as some experience in consciousness, but as Consciousness.

As the Self is unfolding itself to itself, from within itself, you will have all these realizations of a transcendental nature, that you are the state of Being itself.

When you graduate into the actual, embodied fullness of meditation, then the Divine has adopted your life. The Divine Consciousness has then swallowed you. Then it speaks its truth as your existence, as your life.

So, as you can imagine, every conceivable fear will arise in that process. You will have the fear of being extinguished forever or the fear that you may never be extinguished.

You will be backed into a corner where everything about you comes under scrutiny, the scrutiny of Consciousness itself, to reveal the whole nature of human functioning, the whole nature of the urge toward survival, the urge toward pleasure, the urge toward pain and its avoidance. Everything will be brought into this magnified perception in the present moment. In this present moment everything becomes stark and real for the first time.

To be thrust from the conceptual into the Real is the essence of the awakened life. It is one thing to be Self-Realized. It is still another to be given the Awakened Heart Consciousness.

Self-Realization is an empty barrel and the Awakened Heart Consciousness is like a barrel swirling with Light, Bliss and Energy. It is a state of being intoxicated in God, of abiding in God-Consciousness.

The more you have drunk of this inner emptiness, this void-consciousness, this state of eternal nothingness, the deeper that has gone into you, the more profoundly you may become inebriated later on in the resuscitated condition of the Awakened Heart.

Self-Realization is non-incarnated Bliss and the Awakened Heart Consciousness—in the Divine Mother—is incarnated Bliss-Consciousness.

*The Essence of the Real, May 7, 2002, DVD #W-2*

# Meditation in the Unconditioned Space of the Heart Provokes Purification in the Body-Mind

The atmosphere is so subtle, so quiet. To feel spaciousness is to feel meditation, which brings you the deep, peaceful atmosphere of no-activity, no-mind.

The human nervous system enjoys meditation because it reconnects us with the essence of who we are. It brings us into the unconditioned space of the Heart. In this atmosphere, something special starts to happen, a spontaneous occurrence within consciousness.

Usually we feel separate from everything. We think of everything as something other, something different than what we are. But in this atmosphere it's as if we all arise together in the same Universal Consciousness. We share a sacred dimension of togetherness. We don't quite know how that happens. It's something that is revealed, something that is felt, something that may be known on the inside. As we remain in this atmosphere, we begin to open up like a flower. There's something all-pervasive, all-permeating, massive, that actually arises when we sit here together. I don't know how else to express it. It's not the by-product of any kind of belief or system of thinking. It's not the result of any effort. It doesn't happen because of anything else. It happens because we're in an atmosphere of reciprocal perception. We perceive each other in this Ocean of Consciousness, that's already active. The intention of my sitting here is not to create something. It's just to remember something already present. It's already there. You could say it's being invoked, summoned, stimulated and that's enough for it to respond. It responds of its own nature.

I'm not doing something with my emotions or my mind to create it. I'm just here with you, easily functioning, and as a result this Consciousness begins to become awakened, it comes to be released into the atmosphere.

If you have, say, gotten used to an atmosphere where there was insufficient oxygen, somehow your system would adapt to that. You wouldn't be living from the level of your total potential. You wouldn't be feeling your full aliveness, because your breathing capacity would be reduced as a result of the lack of oxygen. It's the same way in here. We come into this atmosphere and each one of us is coming from a particular place, and it may not have been the best atmosphere, the one that's most suitable to living in an expanded state of consciousness. But we adapt. We adapt to wherever we happen to be, so that we can live day to day.

What we call purification is when your body begins to break the habit of old adaptation and rises to meet a higher vibration, a higher vibrational quality that it has not yet integrated into. It has not yet fused into this higher level of living or aliveness and therefore there's a kind of lag that happens. The body-mind has to catch-up to this heightened awareness and we call that purification. We call that evolution, spiritual evolution.

So, if you've been deprived of full oxygen and all of a sudden you're in an atmosphere of total oxygen, or at least the amount you're supposed to have, then you may actually go into a state of vertigo or imbalance, due to the influx of purity, the purity of that atmosphere. In the same way, you could come and sit here and as a result of being in this refined atmosphere, you may for a moment get thrown "off balance." But you're being thrown off your old balance into a new equilibrium, a more profound harmony, which has more of the Shakti, more of the Universal Energy in it, the Universal Vibration.

What happens is that you begin to re-own your higher dimension of functioning when you come here. You begin to re-integrate back into a higher level of wakefulness. They call it enlightenment. You become enlightened here. You become suffused in this quality because it is spontaneously being stimulated, invoked; and it arises. It actually starts to move in waves.

You may ask, "Where does it come from?" Well, it's hard to say. Does it come from within me? Sort of. Does it come from you? Sort of. Does it come from something that's beyond both of us? Yes, sort of. Does it really reside anywhere? It resides everywhere. It resides in everything. Somehow though, we're capable of stimulating That in itself. That Life-Energy can be provoked. It can be excited. It can be stimulated into more vibrancy, more power. Shakti means power.

So, when I'm talking to you, I'm not really talking to you. I'm really talking to That. You'll feel that if you're really paying attention. That way I can just come from that purity. We can remain in this simple absorption of the present moment.

As a result of getting an exposure to That, something may happen inside you. You may say, "Wow, this feels different than where I was just an hour ago. This is totally different."

It is and it isn't, you know. You're carrying this within you. It's just that it's now coming awake.

*Breathing in Consciousness, April 12, 2003, DVD #4*

# Descent into Language

We can only go downhill from here. There's nothing that can clarify, or elucidate, or give more meaning to existence than meditation. So we're about to take a descent into language.

Descent doesn't mean "bad." It just means that we're flowing down into a field of constriction. We're so expanded in meditation—either we dissolve, or we ascend, or we descend into a Limitless Feeling. Whereas, once we start to cognize and verbalize, we move in the opposite direction.

Both are full. That is full and this is full. They're two different kinds of fullnesses. When we have just the fullness of meditation, the subjective dimension has been expanded into Consciousness. The other fullness is the unbearableness of change, the power of the Shakti, which is Feeling—that which wants to expand itself in the field of love and manifestation.

So the first fullness results in detachment, subsiding into the inner witness, the indweller: Atman, Pure Consciousness, the Self. And the other is enjoying the play of relativity.

So, if there are two fullnesses, what is sorrow? There are these two superlatives that just exist next to each other, parallel to each other, the fullness of Silence and the fullness of action. Then, what is sorrow?

Sorrow is the imaginary concept of the "me" that sees both of those things. All you have is that Silence and the fullness of change. Both are limitless and they go on forever.

*Inwardness and Beyond, May 13, 2003, DVD #W-3*

## Action and Meditation

Life can become problematic when there is too much meditation or there's too much action.

Either one can bring a host of problems.

When one becomes attached to detachment, in meditation, problems arise.

When one becomes attached to action, to change, problems arise.

So there is a kind of free-flowing beauty that exists, that unites these two.

*Inwardness and Beyond, May 13, 2003, DVD #W-3*

# Release Arising Sensations and Images and Enjoy the Return to Presentness

*Participant:* I also feel a strong pulling feeling in my chest. It's getting really hot! Why?

*David:* I'm not sure I can tell you why. There are many experiences that many people have here and they are wide-ranging. Each experience is right for each person. But again, it's difficult to say what every experience is.

I would suggest though, that no matter what experience arises, let your attention also fall back upon the nature of your mind, on the nature of mind itself, in other words, on the background in which every experience is occurring. Just randomly, scan your awareness, see what your whole awareness *is*, the whole feeling of Being. Even while these experiences are going on, try to get a sense of the whole feeling, the whole of you, what that is in terms of what is being experienced. If you get too fixated on an individual experience, it will eat up your attention.

There will be all sorts of symptoms that arise in you, which give evidence that something different is happening here, that this is an occasion where Life moves, Energy moves, consciousness is affected. And so, knowing there's a big picture here pay attention to everything, both to what's happening in experience and where you reside as a whole.

*Orley:* To illustrate that, David, a viewer says that there's a burning in the chest, a deep sense of penetration, an image of a skull and cracking of bones in the skull.

*David:* So yes, images too can arise, images which are symbols. Again, I don't advise focusing too deeply on this and treating it like an academic exercise, or as an exercise in which we're studying how to look at dreams or images coming into consciousness spontaneously. Rather, notice these things and really release them, and then breathe back into the sensation of being present, enjoying the return to presentness, to presence, to Being, and see what you learn from that. Just take it slowly and treat this as an exercise in attention, rather than focusing into content with the goal of understanding something.

*Talks and Dialog on the Internet, Volume 3, December 16, 2008*

## Stay out of the Role of Self-Controlling Censor

*Participant:* As the mind slows and there is a sleepiness, should one fight this with attention or just surrender and allow it?

*David:* It actually could be a very deep meditation dawning in you, so just let the mind drop. Stay seated in a meditative posture, if you can, and just let the mind go, or sink into a deepened feeling, or deepened sense of Being. I don't recommend resisting that, certainly. And see if there's some kind of awakening within the core of the mind. That will determine whether it's meditation or not. Or it may be the beginning of meditation. It might not go so deep as to be described as an awakening at the very core of the mind. But it will definitely inform you that it's something evolutionary, that it's something positive in terms of meditation.

The key is to just remain innocent. Refrain from self-correcting when you're here. If self-criticism comes up while you're here, just let it be part of the ongoing flow of experience. If something negative arises, like judgment or criticism, self-criticism, criticism of me, criticism of someone perhaps in your life that you're not even with now, just let it arise in Consciousness. Let it arise, let it blossom, and then let it go its way, so that you stay out of the role of self-controlling censor. You don't want to censor. And during that time you may become aware of the activity of Spiritual Transmission, and it's very precious to notice that and to come to an appreciation of that activity.

*Talks and Dialog on the Internet, Volume 3, December 16, 2008*

# Enlightenment Is the Death of Fun, so Let's Stay Here a Little Bit, so We Can Enjoy Each Other

*Participant:* I just want to say that I don't think I've ever felt such stillness in this room.

*David:* People are not even breathing.

*Participant:* Right.

*David:* This is what I want to do with you. This is what I wanted to share with you. I believe this is the evolutionary force of the universe we're tasting together. It's wonderful, wonderful, wonderful, wonderful, like an exotic garden. You're just in this exotic place now, this primeval forest.

Meditation comes easy in this environment—just go within. I'm not supposed to be disturbing you, please forgive me. I'm supposed to be conducive to that which is happening in you now. But I'm beginning to feel a little abandoned up here all by myself [smiling]. I'm having my "abandonment issues" come up.

Do you feel the Spiritual Potency? Do you feel this? What is it for you? Tell me what it is. How are you experiencing it?

*Participant:* A vibration and vibrancy.

*David:* Yes, that's beautiful. It's real, isn't it?

*Participant:* Oh, yes!

*David:* This is what I mean by Transmission. Now you're becoming vividly aware of some very pure aspect of that Field, yes, and your body, your whole body-mind complex is connecting right there with it.

*Participant:* It can be experienced on a cellular level as well.

*David:* Right, or just on a Consciousness level. You can just feel revitalized and expanded in your awareness, like the way everyone was falling into meditation. I pulled you out. But if I had left you there you'd just keep going into the Void. But why attain enlightenment? [Smiling] Let's hang out together.

*Participant:* It's so much fun.

*David:* Enlightenment is the death of fun, the death of all fun.

15

So let's stay here a little bit, so we can enjoy each other. You don't want to become "too enlightened!"

*Love, Growth and Evolution March 4, 2011, DVD #35*

# The Only Way to Relinquish Fear-Based Consciousness Is to Merge into the Consciousness That Meditation Offers

In meditation, those things that differentiate us from one another fall away. What remains is common to all of us: Universal Consciousness, Pure Consciousness.

Meditation is extremely precious, for it draws the individual consciousness, the differentiated will, into the Void. It draws the psychology out of its fixation with differences, distinctions, and delivers it into a relaxed area. That process of releasing the individual mind into the Cosmic Silence educates the mind to relax its uptightness. It instructs the mind on how to become tolerant. So, you can see how precious meditation is.

Without understanding what meditation is, a human being will remain bound and miserable. It doesn't matter what the content of his life is. If he doesn't actually undergo the process of releasing his self-consciousness into Universal Being, he will feel claustrophobic, or she will feel denied access to real happiness. Again, I want to stress that meditation is an existential, and not a spiritual, or even a religious practice. It's an absolutely natural, native encounter with one's Self.

And the beauty of meditation is that it invites the human being to become ripe, to bring about a kind of emotional, psychological, fruition. And it does this precisely by taking the being out of the arena of social, political, economic, and environmental concerns. It draws away from those concerns, which suffocate the mind's natural ability to expand.

The concept of God is a very deceptive term. The idea that God is a somebody is not only incorrect, it's dangerous. Religion gives birth to this misunderstanding that God is something different, something somewhere else, something other than what one is.

But that which is called God is reached only through meditation. Even prayer cannot bring you into the arena of God-Consciousness. Prayer remains in the field of duality and therefore is insufficient to bring one to the doorstep of what is called God, which is a state of Being.

So, what is this state of Being, which meditation draws us into, that religion calls God? What is the essence of this plane of existence? In a sense, it's a dimension where everything that can and will happen to you has already happened. It's a place that takes you out of linear time and into a different appreciation of existence.

In time and space, the human mind becomes acclimated to functioning in boundaries. Yet between each boundary, between the beginning and ending of each event in experience, is a gap of nothingness, a point of emptiness. That point is God. That point is the essence of a human being's being. And contact with that point radically transforms the nature of a human existence. It drives the human being into a higher field of knowing, an all-inclusive kind of perception that definitely negates the time-bound, space-bound mind that lives in boundaries.

Real meditation is an act of negation. The effect, the profound consequence of true meditation, is a tremendous act of negation. It's a funneling, a pooling, of all the energies and capacities of the human being, drawing them into a singular mode of perception.

A human being who is able to meditate naturally, spontaneously, drawing the mind into that field of absolute negation, someday encounters the most radical human event, the most radical event that can be experienced in a human birth, which is the climax of individual consciousness into Transcendental Reality.

I'm referring here to the final fracturing of the conditioned personality that is put together through thought, experience and sensation. The fracturing of that solid entity, and the simultaneous opening of awareness into the Absolute, describe the final pinnacle of human experience. It is the purpose of a human birth, the purpose of life, of living.

That fracturing of the individual personality into the Silence has dramatic consequences. It opens the human being to a kind of experience that begins to reverberate with extraordinary Universal Power. Whereas the time-bound, space-bound consciousness functions in a tiny arena of cause and effect, this other kind of mind functions within the very Source-Matrix of existence. It's thinking out of the same Field that animals and insects, mammals, birds, all living things think out of, function out of, live out of. A human being who lives in that kind of Reality has become radically exposed to the natural consciousness of Unity.

He or she is born into a kind of functioning that we see going on in the natural world.

Contrary to what religions have taught us, that the religious mind is somehow one that rises above the natural world and finds a truth that is in contradiction to everything that you see and experience, the true and correct understanding of spiritual life is that the human being literally breaks down, dissolves, so that she can then begin to breathe uninhibitedly in the natural consciousness of the Organic World.

So, life is not about being "saved." It's not about being "redeemed." Those are a few men's hallucinations. What we are talking about is a genuine, intuitive grasping of the highest principle of existence: that the natural world is in-breathing us, that we breathe into this natural climate of Organic Wholeness, and it breathes us.

Having found that kind of connection, a remarkable thing can then begin to happen. All of the latent frequencies of intelligence in nature can become available to an individual human mind. The time-bound, space-bound mind, which functions in synthetic, man-made concepts cannot grasp this understanding: that *nature itself begins to think the human being.*

At this point something very interesting can happen. The human being can begin to construct a real human civilization, based on true intelligence, native organic intelligence. You can see what a radical breakage this is from the conditioned mind of the ordinary human being. You can appreciate what a drastic departure this is from what we call human civilization and human culture.

The fear that you see exemplified in religious followers comes from the sensation of duality. It comes from the sensation that "I" am different from this world. "I" am different from you. "I" am different from the universe or the cosmos. Wherever that difference exists, you have a fear-based existence, a human existence that is bound interminably and eternally to fear and violence. So, the only way to relinquish that fear is to merge into the consciousness that meditation offers. There is no other way. Reading spiritual books will inevitably lead to obstinate conclusions about what you think you've realized.

Religion is a dead end. The very unfortunate thing is that whenever a human being suppresses his natural impulses and surrenders himself to something outside of himself in order to attain peace, he simultaneously generates hate. Suppression, fear, hate, violence, control, separation are all part of a single consciousness and it is precisely that consciousness that is undone through meditation.

A miraculous field is birthed when you start putting together one or more human beings who have fratured their relationship with finite existence, who are enlightened. These beings begin to multiply the power of Organic Consciousness. They begin to expand and transcend all limitations in thought and feeling, and a beautiful human culture can be established, on that basis, when there are enough of these beings functioning. That is what meditation offers.

*Meditation and Religion, June 4, 2005, DVD #9*

Joshua Tree National Park

You have to have a big heart for this venture. You can't be afraid. You have to be really certain about what you want. There's no room for hesitation, except maybe at the beginning. Once you start to get a taste, then it's too late. Once you know that happiness, it's too late. You've got to take it to the end.

part [2]

Non-Duality

Joshua Tree National Park

# When You Stop Managing Your Consciousness, You'll Realize You Have Nothing

When you stop managing your consciousness, you'll realize then you have nothing, you own nothing. You don't even own your own process of going beyond. You can't even do that. Nor can you hold onto the Absolute once it apparently goes. So you're in the same boat. You have nothing. You are nothing. So get used to the feeling of being nothing, being nobody. That's the jewel. That's the precious jewel. That's what allows you to go on and get the highest unity and then not even be moved by that.

You can't take God from God. You can't add God on to God. So you stay unmoved through the whole process. You become utterly released from, utterly indifferent to, your own spiritual process and that's real liberation. That's liberation from liberation. That's freedom from freedom.

Then, don't ask in the end, who you are or who you are not, whether you're form or whether you're formless. It's all happening as you and even that's just an idea, just an expression, a verbal equivalency of something you can't describe. So, in a very real sense, there's no knowledge in any of this. It's not about acquiring knowledge. Knowledge will just keep separating you out from the knower and you're back in that boat of separation.

The full potency of the Absolute is here now. It's thrilled. It's happy. It's not happening for anybody. It's not happening through anybody.

*An Evening of Dialog, October 9, 2009, DVD #25*

# Advaita, Devotion, and the Transcendence of All Concepts

Advaita looks so charming because it looks sanitary. It looks hygienic. There's no individuality in it. There's "nobody" there to deceive you. But, how can you say that when advaita is always delivered through a human being? It came about through human culture, through human minds. Advaita was invented by the human intellect. The whole concept of it—even non-dualism—is a concept. So, when you start questioning that concept, now you're getting to the real foundations of advaita, when you describe the form or package in which it comes wrapped.

I've never said advaita Vedanta is not worth knowing. I always praise it. How can you not praise the Non-Dual? How can you say anything bad about the One?

Yet there's been a great misunderstanding in the juxtaposition of jnana yoga with the whole topic of advaita Vedanta.

Nisargadatta, one of the big voices of non-dualism in Indian philosophy—of advaita Vedanta—performed puja to his teachers in the morning. So, if it's so bereft of bhakti, why would he do that and why would he sing bhajans with people?

Once you make the distinction between advaita Vedanta and jnana yoga, that jnana yoga is used *as a means* to attain advaita Vedanta, then you can now appreciate that advaita Vedanta belongs to every spiritual lineage, so long as they're taken to the end, to the end and beyond. Which is what? It is the Field where you can't construct anything mentally about what you've experienced. You are beyond the mind totally.

*Discussing Advaita, October 10, 2009, DVD #26*

## Self-Inquiry Is a Hot Penetration into the Subterranean Levels of Consciousness

Many people think Self-inquiry is a very analytical kind of thing, like you're actually doing a mathematical equation or something like that—that we're just figuring something out about the nature of the "I," and then you understand it. It's really a deconstruction of the entire structure of the ego, due to a hot penetration down into the subterranean levels of consciousness, the subjectivity, and then through the subconscious, through the unconscious, the pre-conscious and then into the transcendent, totally prior Consciousness of Cosmic Being.

When something becomes relevant to you, directly relevant to you as an individual, and passion is brought into the process, it's not just mechanical study. It's not just the intellect operating on its own. There's this fiery Love-Pressure that's introduced into the inquiry, where it's almost like you're pushed to the edge of what you can tolerate. You're learning how to expand your level of tolerance itself, what you can explore with the entire force of your being, and that's real jnana, which is bhakti, isn't it?

And it's also fueled by raw feeling. You can't keep your heart out of the process. You can't keep your feeling-nature out of it, somehow segregated and put on hold, while you

27

do the "real work," which is done by the mind. They come together. They fuse into a synergistic combination that's lethal for limited existence. You can then incinerate from within.

I had to stay in a perpetual state of Self-inquiry when I was at Clark University doing my undergraduate work. Those years were hot with extraordinary inquiry into the nature of Being, all the while getting deep transcendental experiences in meditation, but then just passing through them, leaving them from where they came, not attaching at all.

I knew I had to keep moving until it wasn't possible to move any longer. I knew I had to take it to the end. I didn't know what I'd find there or what that would be like. I just knew that the whole process would be extinguished. But, I didn't know what that entailed. I just had to walk that walk, like many of you are doing here.

*Discussing Advaita, October 10, 2009, DVD #26*

# I Never Distinguish Myself Apart from Anything

*David:* There's a constant stream of Bliss-Filled Consciousness, which is arising, transmitting, entering into other beings, helping, helping constantly without question and answer, without even asking for it.

*Swami-G:* Absolutely. But, it's not something that some persona, a teacher, is going to force to happen. You can block the Transmission. You have free will. You can choose to not open yourself to it, and you can have it blocked, or it can work on a subtle level.

*David:* No outer authority. It's authorityless.

*Swami-G:* Yes, it just takes place. It's that love, that Divine Love that's just there. It just happens in flow. So one gives what can be given. Then, it's up to the sadhaka, what they do with it or not. People don't understand that they choose their suffering out of ignorance, because they don't know the difference.

*David:* Don't you think, though, that even suffering is an organic event in nature, in that, if something isn't right, it just needs more time on its own to come to its own fruition? Do you think that suffering is deliberately self-perpetuated in an individual?

*Swami-G:* No. It's done out of ignorance.

*David:* It *is* ignorance. For me, I'm still in ignorance. There's no difference. What is ignorance? Where is it? Show it to me. And yet, there's this whole subject-object world. This is real. So, in ignorance you're in a cycle of complete acting out all the time, without a break.

*Swami-G:* Exactly. You don't know the way out. You don't know the roadmap out, and you don't understand that you're re-victimizing yourself—and that you are the one, the key, to come out of it, as well. You have the key to come out of it.

*David:* Because so many seekers and aspirants are pitting themselves against this thing called ignorance! One of the first proclamations I make in my sittings is that I'm completely ignorant and I'm just like you. Now, can we just relax, please? That there's no difference on that level between us.

*Swami-G:* Yeah. No, there is no difference.

*David:* And, where else would ignorance be? It would be in the Self! It's the maya. It's the mayic aspect that gives rise to all these forms. That's its measurement. It's the mind of measurement. It's the reality of delineation and quantification. It has no independent existence. But yet, I have separate hands. I have separate eyes. If I have a tooth-ache, I go to the dentist. I don't say "it's maya." So, I suffer. I am suffering. I never distinguish myself apart from any-thing, from any level of experience or even perception. I tell people: I am ego. Why are you running away from it? Let's just sit and be friends in that ego. The ego wants chocolate. It wants peanut butter. Give it what it wants—just don't eat hydrogenated peanut butter!

*Swami-G:* Okay. So, but when you use the term ego then— and I think we have a different usage of it again—for you, the ego is the illusion of being that suffering mind.

*David:* Yes. Yes.

*Swami-G:* And when Realization takes place, you're no longer ego, because you have no illusion that you are some separate persona. That persona has ended.

*David:* The feeling of that separative identity has been melted away.

*Swami-G:* Exactly, so that's why I say there is no longer ego. I'm not saying that within That there's not something that's still interacting in the world. There is still something that's interacting in the world.

*David:* Absolutely. And memory is involved, correct?

*Swami-G:* Ahh, well. I can't say that too much for here. There's not too much memory.

*David:* I understand. I understand. But, when someone calls your name, you respond correctly?

*Swami-G:* Yes, of course, of course.

*David:* So, there's some memory there. In a given instance, it's all empty.

*Swami-G:* Exactly.

*David:* And, short-term memory seems to get you by. It's like, if it goes a little beyond that point, it's quite empty.

*Swami-G:* It's gone. It's gone.

*David:* Ramakrishna described his teaching as being in a "mansion of fun." And I thought that's a delicious description, both of the enormity of it and the fact that even there, where there are great samadhis, great erasures of personal consciousness, permanently established voidness, sahaja samadhi in the end, you can just laugh and joke with people. You can be a friend. You can be happy. You can cry with people.

*Swami-G:* Exactly. You're with people on their level. Wherever they come to, that's what plays out. That's all.

*David:* The Lila-Shakti of That.

*Swami-G:* Exactly, of whatever it is.

*David:* Even ignorance is just a playing out of this Ultimate Truth.

*Swami-G:* Exactly.

*David:* When people come to me, they say, "I'm ignorant." I say to them, "I don't believe you. But we'll have this discussion if you want to."

*Swami-G:* And that's fine.

*David:* Of course, you have to just love people where they are.

*Swami-G:* Well, exactly.

*David:* It's that unconditional acceptance that gives birth to the trust that you can then illustrate the Enlightened Mind.

*Swami-G:* Exactly.

*Swami-G and David, May 3, 2010*

# The Transition from "I Am That" to "Thou Art That" and "Everything Is That"

Self-Realization is the stage of life in which you realize that your Consciousness is beyond the world of form. It is immersed in formless Being, the Absolute. This is the first phase of realization.

There is a more mature swing within that initial tendency toward the Un-Manifest that pushes toward the outer reality, what we call the external world. The immature phase of Self-Realization insists that "I am That" and that's the end of the story. It does not contain the knowledge that "Thou art That" and "Everything is That." Those two latter movements belong to a more mature phase of Self-Realization.

So, the initial phase is exclusive. It's exclusively subjective. It's merely a statement of the subjective terrain or depth of one's own Consciousness. Whereas, this latter movement is more on a horizontal plane, which begins to embrace the outer forms and states of being that exist within the world. Included within those states of being are also your dream state, your sleep state, and your waking state. Those too become embraced in this more advanced form of Self-Realization.

When you hear the words of the Realized speak about

Self-Realization it sounds easy, as though it's the most obvious and undeniable of all realities, that it's more obvious even than the perception of the world. But on its own level the mind struggles deeply to actually surrender into that reality. It's usually a long, drawn-out affair.

The bridge between the difficult and the easy is the teacher. It's in tuning your mind to the teacher's mind, which is the Self, so that your self can also become transcendentally educated and then, later on, undergo the more embracing phase of Full Self-Realization.

The teacher, the living embodiment of the teacher, the Radiation Power of the teacher's Self, is what can help those who are not yet educated fully in the Self. It's a total education and that *existence* is what is learned, not some piecemeal knowledge.

The whole is learned in terms of what one truly is, not mere adoption of scriptural injunctions, faith in God, etc., but something more drastically intimate.

*Widening Self-Realization, February 19, 2010, DVD #31*

# Real Awakening Is a Mysterious Place of Unknowingness—the Heart Itself

You see, anything that you can experience is not real awakening. Real awakening is a mysterious place of unknowingness, that is, the very Heart itself, and it never becomes objectified in any experience.

At the same time, the field of experience does go through a series of transformations to the Self, in the field of perception and knowledge, which indicates that a process is, or has been going on, that indicates total enlightenment.

Gradually, you return to a kind of pristine innocence in your human dimension after all these phases have phased out, these phases of awakening. You return to a state of simple functioning, which is neither ignorant nor awakened.

Please listen very carefully to this. The state that you return to has no quality to it. It's not ecstatic. It's not inebriated. It's not illumined. It's not attached. It's not not-attached. So, be very careful here. You can't say it's this and it's not that. You can't say, "This is present in the enlightened state, but that's not."

In the final state everything is simultaneously transcended and embraced, not deliberately, not with the will, not with the intellect or the mind or the senses. It simply is a non-reaction. It's a no-reaction to a no-state in a no-arena.

So, what *is* there is something that simply lingers. That is your very Self. You can't explain it to anyone. You would just sound like an idiot if you tried to explain it in words.

It's something that doesn't indicate holiness or sinfulness. It doesn't indicate virtue or vice. It doesn't indicate any particular quality of having arrived at any particular realization, except you can say that you, or your potentiality, have been totally transformed into Life itself, that you are lived by Life.

All the indications are there that life has subsumed you, devoured you, absorbed you, and that what remains is Consciousness-Only, or Life-Only—an organism functioning in an organic wholeness. A state of mind would ensue, which treasured and enjoyed the world of nature. This state of mind would be drastically turned-off to the domination of the human being over nature, and of the corporate mentality over the rest of the world—the corporate consciousness of bargaining-trading, buying and selling, owning and renting. All of that is very obnoxious to the relaxed state of sahaja samadhi.

You can't use anyone or anything, at that point, for your ultimate purposes. You've been released into the most primal, exquisite innocence of Being itself, which can't put anything between you and the other. It cannot erect any sense of forced usefulness.

So, at that point, this miraculous human being has transcended the need for any kind of religious or spiritual instruction. He or she relies totally on a direct, organic connection with the intelligence of Life itself, with Nature itself, to execute actions.

*Self-Realization and Awakening, May 7, 2005, DVD #7*

# "I Don't Know" Is Perfection, "I Know" is Disaster

When you learn to say, "I don't know," like a little child, you're instantaneously open and liberated. "I don't know" is perfection. "I know" is disaster.

You can only see that you don't know when everything is going wrong in your life. If you're still hit or miss and some things are going right and some things are going wrong, you might be tempted into thinking that you still might be doing something right. But when everything falls apart, that's the true fertile state.

So, you can't really sell this kind of thing. No one would buy their own destruction. Only to someone who's madly in love with existence can destruction appear to be something nectarous, something to be craved. Then, you will say, along with the poet, "What destruction am I blessed by."* Then you will say: my annihilation creates me.

So naturally, as you progress on this path and you truly awaken you become crazy and the world, which once appeared to be so sealed in certainty, now has all kinds of glaring cracks of inconsistency.

So, you're here to pay the ultimate price with your life. It's the sacrifice, the offering of your entire life into that initial meditative awakening, which catapults you into the beyond forever—in this body, in this world; not after you die. There's no "after."

There's nothing that comes after anything else. Sequences

and endings and beginnings are all terminated. They are off-limits. Then you live in the simple aridity of honesty and surrender.

*Into the Beyond, March 18, 2002, DVD #21, * A.R. Ammons*

# The Only Time You Can Manifest Correct Functioning Is without a Belief System, When You Look with Empty Eyes

When the philosophical minds that love teleological explanations (explanations which point toward a goal) get hold of the idea of enlightenment, they make it sound as if enlightenment is the means to some higher end for the human race. It is not. That's simply a very over-masculinized interpretation.

This is something you see in the human being that you don't see too much in the animal kingdom: the ability to go into a very high mental plane and engage in fantasies that are self-destructive, especially in the field of religious belief where thought worships thought, where the image making process worships the image making process. And so you see that's samsara, that's eternal damnation, to use their term. That's the wheel of endless suffering, when human beings become victim to their own incorrect functioning. The only time you can manifest correct functioning is without a belief system, when you look with empty eyes.

Theology, philosophy, metaphysics are all mental recreation. All those systems of thought are not to be taken seriously.

They can be talked about and debated, but then there should be this placid sense of nothingness that's self-apparent, that prevents the human being from getting seriously involved with potentially destructive belief systems.

So, when we talk about spiritual awakening, we mean someone who has shattered the essence of their own capacity for negative functioning. An awakened human being has eradicated a certain way of knowing or propensity to know. Something happens to the brain when awakening shatters. Something occurs in the nervous system to change the functioning of that nervous system, forever.

And the person to whom that's happened is like a freak in this world, from a functional point of view. He is not functioning in the same manner as the ordinary human being. It's absolutely different—not higher, not better, not holier. It is absolutely, distinctively, qualitatively different.

It's only the person who has realized That and lives it involuntarily that can talk about it, someone who no longer has any choice in the matter, and whose subtlest mind has been eradicated, so that there is no-mind left. Then, in that innocent expansion, energies arise. You can call them subtle beings, deities, frequencies of nature, energetic patterns. You can call them whatever you want. They begin to descend into that Being and live there and function out of That.

The Awakened Being becomes like a tower, a radio tower, transmitting and receiving all kinds of subtle frequencies, perceptions, revelations. It is not so much that he communicates the individuated aspect of those things. He is something beyond all of them into which they all aggregate. He is the flower and then all of these bees come. He is the Flower that's opened and then the various bees of Energy, Light,

Exhilaration, and Emptiness come in and draw the nectar out of That, and fly away and give it out to everything.

Something much more than a talk is happening here as this Self-Generating Bliss occurs spontaneously.

*Animated by Enlightenment, November 5, 2002, DVD #19*

## Only through Feeling-Consciousness Can You Satisfy Both the Urge to Know and the Urge to Feel

To speak *about* Consciousness is an intellectual exercise, but to speak *in* Consciousness is a devotional one. To speak in Consciousness requires that the separate sense, or the separate self, bow down into Consciousness.

To talk about Consciousness yields knowledge, but to talk within Consciousness produces the feeling of Being, or of Consciousness itself. The former path leads to discursive knowledge, which increases the sense of distance between the subject and Consciousness, whereas devotional speech increasingly immerses itself in Consciousness. One path leads to speculation and the other path leads to inebriation.

No amount of knowledge about Consciousness will satisfy the yearning for it. But just a little taste of the feeling of it will produce a great sense of satisfaction. To taste the actual energy of Consciousness, as it's moving within itself, satisfies the eternal hunger in the human being. It is coming home. It is feeling as though one has arrived at that place, which generates the longing to love and be loved, and the juxtaposed longing to know everything.

Only through Feeling-Consciousness can you satisfy both of those urges, the urge to know and the urge to feel. Once you can feel Consciousness, as it begins to disperse throughout your entire being, you then can begin to look through Consciousness, touch through Consciousness, know through Consciousness, hear through Consciousness.

When all of those avenues are rooting back to the Self, the Transcendental Being, then Oneness occurs and one has the cognition of Everlasting Life, of the First Beginning, the origin and home of the entire human journey, the evolutionary journey of this planet, of this world and all the other worlds.

The unique gift of a human nervous system affords that experience. So, this human embodiment is holy, sacred, divine, perfect. It is God. It is the manifestation of the Lord, the Lord of the Cosmos, the Lord that exists beyond duality—the Heart. To speak *in* Consciousness is to bleed Consciousness, to bleed it out of the body-mind and into the atmosphere, where the fragrance of that Bliss can be absorbed by other living things, by everything, by everyone.

If you look very closely at the awakening process, the very state of awakening—and by look I mean to simply abide in with caring, caringness, and listeningness, listening to the sound of that Silence, that inner awakening—you might begin to intuit that in the natural state of sahaja samadhi there is no longer any center of the human personality. There is no inner fulcrum that we call "the center." The center has been removed. There is no place to reflect back onto, even to a so-called "Divine Center." This is the true freedom, which can be called no-abidance, non-abiding, or ever-abidingness with "what is." It is Consciousness resting in itself, enjoying the beauty of its own fabric, the depth of its own inwardness.

Having no center yields a particularly inebriating realization, that not only is there nothing to realize, but there is nothing to hold onto, either on the inside or the outside. So whatever you do hold onto, on the outside, is simply done out of human need, simple human need, expediency, sanity in living. But on the inside there is an ever flowing river that rests nowhere, that holds no ultimate knowledge of freedom or liberation: and thus the final relaxation, beyond states, beyond even wanting to become free.

Regardless of what path you are travelling, what sadhana you practice, what your spiritual disposition is, it is indeed possible to come to this fruition with the help, with the aid, of someone who has travelled the entire gamut, who has journeyed the entire process from avidya (ignorance) to Self-Realization, and then from Self-Realization back into the natural state, which is completely free of any claims toward awakening or non-awakening—that place in which limitation and freedom dance a single dance, where bondage and freedom move in and out of one another, in some kind of mysterious conjunction.

So, it doesn't matter what path you travel, as long as it's travelled with sincerity, innocence, trust, love, and humility. Those energies will work upon your path and purify it. The various releases in consciousness, the satories, the breakthroughs into pre-cognitive awareness, may occur repeatedly and over time so that there is eventually a permanent delivery or doorway into the Beyond.

To enter and exit the Beyond will fix you in That, releasing all of your inborn hungers to the Divine in a revitalized form. After that, it's simply a self-generating Self-Knowledge, an intoxicating process of fulfilling all the innate hungers toward transcendental experience until the body-mind becomes so saturated with insight that it's delivered to the point of view where there is no-delivery, no-deliverer, no-freedom and no-bondage—the natural state.

But it's your process to come upon and there's no authority anywhere who can replace your own knowledge about how to undergo this event. There's no knowledge that can substitute the living into it. It is to be lived into, not hoped for, not prayed for.

It is to be the state of your own arrival, through the help and Blessing-Power of fulfillment of that process, whether you call that the Guru, the Master, Life itself, or the inner Self, the inner Guru, whatever you want to call it. That's the true movement of a human birth.

*Knowing Feeling and Non-Abidance, March 7, 2006, DVD #19*

# You Must Have Enough Mindfulness to Be Attentive to the Occasioning of Liberation

Liberation sounds easy and it is easy, but it's not without a challenge of some sort. You must have enough mindfulness to be attentive to the occasioning of liberation. It must be that every human being gets fleeting glimpses of liberation—moksha—throughout a day, thousands of glimpses throughout his or her lifetime, and yet only a few people talk in terms of full knowledge of full awareness. The reason why it's missed is because there's no frame in which to make sense that liberation happens. The frame itself is produced by the dissatisfied mind to hold in view what it currently is not able to understand, which in this case, is liberation.

You can give up this agenda of trying to grasp it, but that does not replace your need to realize it. It is simply not enough to claim a perspective of non-grasping. You have to lie in readiness. You have to always live at the edge of your understanding, at the edge of your mind, which is where this is all glimpsed, or intuited. After a certain amount of constant and uninterrupted glimpsing, you become That, which you've glimpsed—as being beyond yourself, beyond grasping. So then it becomes even more enigmatic. Then it becomes even more paradoxical, what it means to remain steadfastly absorbed in That which is so free. Liberation is not delivered to any aspect of the human being, not even to its intelligence. It escapes the structure of being a state.

*Understanding Liberation, October 13, 2009, DVD #26*

# Are You Disturbed Enough by This Whole Phenomenon of Non-Realization to Start Really Giving Yourself to Your Entire Being?

Just listen. Don't even try to make sense of what I'm saying. Just listen, innocently, just the way a child who doesn't know any language, doesn't have any words, listens to its mother. You see it looking when the mother talks. Yet it has no idea what's being said. It hasn't even formed a single concept in its mind. It's a little crawling thing and yet the mother is saying all these things to it. The baby listens. Have a mind like that, not a sophisticated, cunning human mind all geared up with its purposes, its agendas and its ulterior motives.

It's exciting to consider this possibility, this kind of fabric of understanding. It's exciting because it reminds us of the eternal beauty that we have, that we're really not corrupt, as the religions have said. They all tell you, "you're corrupt." It doesn't matter whether the religions are from the East or the West, from the North or the South. Even the ones that don't talk about good and evil, they invent other words like karma and dharma, bondage, etc. So, you have to have been fed up with all of that before any of this can become understandable. You have to see through the various pitfalls and illusions that have been presented to you by conventional authorities. Otherwise, you haven't inspected the situation in which you yourself were structured—all those ignorant minds that have given birth to all of this ignorance. Well, that's what we've come out of.

There's only one Consciousness. The world is you. If

you're born into an ignorant world, then you were born into that ignorance. It's only your own audacious gesture toward release that has any significance, has any weight to undermine all of that.

If you look at the odds in any life-form manifesting, whether you study mammals, or insects, or plants, there's only a small fraction of a larger possibility that takes successful birth, whether they're crabs or minnows. If you study how these life forms reproduce and put forth future generations, it's only a small, small percentage that actually survive and go on to reproduce. It's the same thing within the human group. Only a small percentage of human beings flower. Yes, many of them take birth, millions upon millions take on bodies, yet only a few flower *within* the human body, flower to the entirety of what their existence is.

These odds should not dissuade you. You shouldn't be diminished morally or in your enthusiasm because the odds are low. If you're wondering why there's so much ignorance on the planet, it's because that's the way nature functions—so many millions upon millions of human beings and so few very realized human beings, who realize what they are, what Consciousness is. It's because that's the way it's supposed to be.

The question is whether you want to be in that game or not, whether you're disturbed enough by this whole phenomenon of non-realization to start really giving yourself to your entire being.

*Understanding Liberation, October 13, 2009, DVD #26*

# You've Got to Know Who You Are, There's No Way around That

We find ourselves here today looking at a very poisoned and ugly world in many ways. You can't rationalize that away with spiritual theories. You can't say reality is essentially Sat-Chit-Ananda and therefore "who cares." That's a deluded, "true believer" talking. You have to face reality.

When you come here, I don't just talk to some essence that wants just Light and Love and Energy. I also talk to you in the context of culture. You can't separate a lot of your miseries from the context in which they have arisen within your culture. But I am a spiritual teacher, so we're going to come out of that, too. I just need to go there with you to remain honest. I don't want to be deceptive or give the impression that I'm avoiding that area of life.

Yet in the context of even this sobering reality, every once in a while Divine Consciousness will capture a human life fully and use that life, regardless of the historical context, to blow through suffering completely, to blow through it unequivocally, to boot it away—and it doesn't have time to fiddle with history.

The key is to access this very powerful state of your own Being and have it wash through you, wash through your intellect and your emotions, and learn to become riveted on That, so That is always speaking to you directly. Then, you'll be very powerful. Then, if you do get up and run for office, and you open your mouth, it will be like a hurricane and people will feel it. They will feel the natural charisma, the Radiant Energy that you are embedded within.

You've got to know who you are. There's no way around that. You've got to find out who you are *as* Consciousness. Forget about history now, we're through with that. You've got to know who you are *in* Consciousness. Otherwise, everything else is going to be cursed. So, to get really deeply into your spiritual wit, you've got to have this touch of anarchy in your psychology. You have to have this touch of revolution going on, revolution from all authority, from every single authority, so that you have the energy to find out what life is.

You've got to be a unique and powerful individual or there's no use in coming here. You've got to embrace yourself in that way, uncompromising. It doesn't mean you can't enter into a surrendered and devotional relationship with me. The kind of devotion that I embody and offer, in spiritual relationship to the people who come to me, is one of full independence, the appreciation of inherent uniqueness within each individual. I possess the sanity never to go in and play with anyone. I leave people to their own lives.

But, have no doubt, what's happening in this room is what every scripture has been written about: in the Upanishads, in what Ramana Maharshi spoke endlessly about. *That* is in this room.

The question is: will you, can you, are you able to come in, in such a way, that we can have a direct and powerful relationship?

You have to have a big heart for this venture. You can't be afraid. You have to be really certain about what you want. There's no room for hesitation, except maybe at the beginning. Once you start to get a taste, then it's too late. Once you know that happiness, it's too late. You've got to take it to the end.

Where does the energy come from to live through this process of Self-Awakening? It does not come from discreet acts of human effort. It does not come from self-willed consciousness. You've got to begin to feel the genuine pulse that's in you. It's there—it's not that far. Once you taste that Energy or that Consciousness, that Silence, you start to get great confidence. You know you can do it, even if you're at the very beginning of the path, even if the mind just comes open a little bit.

When that happens, it's really a whole new birth for you. It's a whole new life. So you begin to follow-up on that. You say, "Wait a minute. What was that remarkable thing that came over me in that instant? It's not characteristic of my life, but it has made a devastating mark on my personality, on my life."

And so you begin to follow-up with that kind of inquiry, which wants to go deeper, and that's the life of sadhana, of living into your spiritual process, until everything goes up into Light.

*Shakti, Embodiment and Non-Duality, September 17, 2010, DVD #32*

# Eventually, This Contrast between the Illusory and the Real Will No Longer Exist

*Orley:* A participant asks, "How does my experience of no-self live alongside the functional self I have in relationship with others? I'm finding this disorienting at times."

*David:* Why is it disorienting?

*Participant:* I am confused about the functional self. It seems like an illusion at times and then it seems quite real.

*David:* The only solution, then, is for everything to become *real*. The dichotomy between the Real and the unreal, the Self and the world, Consciousness and change, is only relevant to a certain level of consciousness.

It's a real duality you're experiencing. That duality between the Real and the illusory is a real dichotomy. It's the only real dichotomy that exists in human experience. So, you need to continue toward a more unified direction, whereby the illusion and the Real bridge

The way that happens is by learning how to live with more and more easiness in the Real. Another thing to remember is that action, or functionality, happens on such a gross level of experience. It always has an illusory quality to it. In other words, keep welcoming the Real, even though it gives rise to this dichotomy. Eventually, a deeper samadhi will be formed, one in which this contrast between the illusory and the Real will no longer exist.

It's really just a process of maturation that I'm describing here. In the forest, the deer gives birth to its baby. When the baby first starts to move, you can be assured that everything is awkward. It's learning how to feel its legs on the ground. It's learning how to walk, to walk faster, to walk with coordination. Eventually, through the process of its own internal maturation and its own physiologic maturation, it learns to just run, and then there's no division between the world and its body. It merges into its environment.

And that too happens in the most mature states of realization, in unity consciousness and sahaja samadhi. When Absolute Being no longer stands out in such grotesque obviousness, the Absolute learns to tolerate the world of change, and thereby absorbs it into its Self.

*An Evening of Dialog, October 9, 2009, DVD #25*

# You Become This Womb-Like Carrier of the Supreme Reality

Until the Paramatman is realized, there is an ascending movement toward That which is above the head, subjectively, which means you are not really interested in the horizontal plane. But, once that has been fully attained in advaitic, Non-Dual Realization, then that vertical current starts to bend.

What happens is that this column-like Energy of Realization, which produces supra-mental and Cosmic Awakening, bends and curves. You cease to be a column, a phallic column, and you become a round, womb-like carrier of the Supreme Reality.

51

*Participant:* Is that what some teachers refer to as the re-generation of the Amrita Nadi?

*David:* Yes, I believe so. You also grow into this further stage. I call it Heart Awakening, Awakened Heart Consciousness. I also call it Divine Mother Consciousness, where the plane of feeling toward objects is both enlightened and still in the field of duality, both at the same time.

By the way, this is just a myth, just a story, too. Don't think this is literal in just the way I say it.

*The Field of Feeling, July 2, 2002, DVD #7*

# The Numbness of Advaitic Self-Realization and the Fullness of the Mother

Advaita turns its back on the world and says there's no world, there's only Self. But that's only because it doesn't have the vast repertoire of enlightened etiquette that the Mother carries. Advaita shies away because it has no way of communicating with all of that chaos. It's quietly blanketed in the numbness of Self-Realization.

How can you express love in such a state? It's insane to even think of how you can have a world of relationships in an advaitic condition. It wouldn't make any sense.

So, the Mother then comes in full form, showering her Grace upon everyone. She wants all her children to be happy. Do you see how different the approach is?

You see, everyone is her child, and she wants to bring fulfillment, Bliss, exhilaration, and joy to all beings, even in the field of death—because every field is a field of death. Wherever she can appear beings will appear and disappear. So, she makes herself known in a field of death and change and mortality. Actually it's her entire playground. So, according to her, she's also in the field of advaita. Nothing really happens anyway!

Her compassion is so tremendous. She has nothing to hold her back. She's crazy. That's why she leaps forth into this whole creation as maya, as the force of world-making. She makes worlds. She's the force of embodiment. So, this whole creation is avataric. It comes out of the Heart of Devi. It comes out of the Heart of the Mother.

I mean, the advaitics have their role, too. Someone has to uphold the truth of no-meaning, no-activity, something that is beyond the field of knowledge. Somebody has to uphold the reality of the screen and its purity. So the advaitics do that.

But Mother has that same knowledge within her and still she jumps into the screen and starts healing things in the movie. You know, it's just what she wants to do. It's Her Lila. It's the Devi Lila.

*The Field of Feeling, July 2, 2002, DVD #7*

# Return Back to the Innocence of the Self

Have you fallen in love with something uncreated? You love it. You can't even say what it is. Yet you're madly in love with it. It's all you think about. It's all you care about. Yet, if you were pressed to give an explanation you would not even know what to say. You'd stumble.

The bhakti path and the jnana path are identical. They lead to the same place. I maintain what Ramana Maharshi maintained, that jnana and bhakti lead to the same condition. They're both implicit within the Self and therefore each is a viable path to the Self; or each is an expression of the presence of the Self. There is no room for many teachings when you are talking about the One. There's only one teaching.

Now, the Self-revealing potency of the Divine is beginning to make itself known. Now, we're getting very intoxicated on God. If you look for it you'll miss it. Just release and stay where you are. Don't do a thing. If you do one thing, you're finished. Then every law in the land will be used against you. If you do one action, you'll be convicted of every crime.

The highest crime is that you may exist. The penalty is death: birth and death. So, think twice before you consider whether you exist or not. You may think it's fun and then you find, "Oh, my God, now I'm born and I have to die, what a bummer." Was it worth existing? Then it's too late. Then you can't get out of this paper bag you've created.

Once you learn the deep lesson of not reacting to your own realization, you're home free; just stay completely removed. Even when the Self comes, ignore it. Act like it's nothing, like it's nobody.

*Participant:* You're reading my mind here.

*David:* Of course. There's only one mind functioning and you're listening—and I'm listening to you. You're listening to me and we're entering into Unity.

*Participant:* There's an amazing clarity all of a sudden!

*David:* Right, lovely, nice and clean, smokeless.

*Participant:* Well, I don't know. Do you get what I'm saying?

*David:* Get it? I am it!

*Participant:* It appears to disappear, and then that's....

*David:* It's an idea. It's an interpretation. That's just the mind rushing in and reacting to its own realization. That's what I'm talking about.

*Participant:* It's rushing in and then it's not rushing in.

*David:* It's like a knee jerk. You can't help it. So you just have to be patient and return back, just toward the innocence of the Self. You're dealing with maya here. This is the supreme trickster of the universe. That thing that's making your mind go is what's making this perceptual realm happen. It's the same trick. It's the same exact trickster. Don't ask me what it is. We just call it maya and we respect it. We bow down to it. We don't consider it as "other" and "evil." Just leave it alone. If you didn't have this body, you wouldn't even be interested in enlightenment, right?

*An Evening of Dialog, October 9, 2009, DVD #25*

# There Are Certain Spiritual Moods That Necessitate Withdrawing from That Discursive, Reasoning Part of the Brain

*Participant:* It's funny. Tonight I can't retain any of the things you're saying at all.

*David:* Tonight?

*Participant:* Yes. I'm hearing them and I can't connect them in a logical sequence at all.

*David:* Yes, I'm having trouble even speaking that way.

*Participant:* Because what's underneath is way stronger.

*David:* Underneath the words? Lovely! There are certain spiritual moods that necessitate withdrawing from the discursive, reasoning part of the brain. That is, if you were to really enforce yourself in that way, you'd actually be detracting from the enlightenment of the moment.

I have faith that whatever happens is the blossoming of a flower. I don't question it. Some nights there will be a great discourse, some nights it will be feeble. Does that make sense? But, do you know the secret of what I do? I remain with "what is," constantly observing internally. I know that the only place that really means something is the subject. It's the subjective dimension.

So, I don't want to *look* good. I don't want to come across as being something special, because that would betray the truth of inwardness. It's beyond inwardness, but we say inwardness just to point in a direction. It's on the outside, too. It spills out from the inside to the outside and then it magnifies itself on the outside, on the external.

Everything is excited about the possibility of the revelation of truth in this moment. It can only occur in this effortless, present moment.

*Inwardness and Beyond, May 13, 2003, DVD #W-3*

## A Silent Fullness That's Welcoming with No Conditions

Just feel in yourself as you are. There's nothing you have to do. There's nothing you have to undo. That's openness. When you realize that, you open. There's nothing to be done, nothing to be undone.

So this is an atmosphere where you breathe in freedom, freedom from the known, freedom from conditioning—from thought, fear, attachment, detachment—freedom from enlightenment. That's joy, Ananda—Bliss.

So we've cut through all those samadhis, fast, all those transcendental awakenings—we cut through them fast. You may say, "But I want to linger. I want to experience that. It's supposed to be so beautiful to have these deep awakenings." It is. But it's better to just be in Bliss, immortal Bliss.

This atmosphere is very unique, a Silent Fullness that's welcoming with no conditions, a Silence that affirms nothing other than itself. It will not affirm some object, some book.

The truth is written in you. Truth was written by you, for you. Truth is not the property of anyone.

*Inwardness and Beyond, May 13, 2003, DVD #W-3*

# We Become Powerless Here, We Move into a Sphere Where There Is No Other

Hopefully, you don't see me as any kind of authority with power—power in what I say or power in what I claim. Hopefully, you don't go there. I stay out of that arena. It's aversive to me to be related to some form of power-domination. I can't imagine it. In fact, we become powerless here. We move into a sphere where there is no other. That's a state of absolute weakness. People don't like words like this because they're generated from an area where there is no sense of separation, and therefore, no ability to control. People get frightened when they can't control. So, if I'm saying you become absolutely weak, you may think I'm talking about some devastatingly negative condition. I am not. I'm talking about something that upholds the innocence of your being, which has no power over anything else, no power over anyone else. Does that make sense?

I get intoxicated when I speak this way, because I'm talking about the essential nature of Being. I'm talking about Consciousness. I'm not talking about an object. The most beautiful thing you can do is to come into this Feeling where your mind has been severed from its tendency to exteriorize, its tendency to create a sense of otherness, and to actually feel its own inner workings—and beyond those workings, the Primal Consciousness of Being itself. We no longer have any need, any fixation for an external deity, an external god. We realize that these are just props created by the mind to, once again, hold itself in a field of subservience and domination. We have no interest in any of that.

We don't want to be right. It's too vulnerable in this condition to even crave the feeling that "I am right." What can you be right about? Who could possibly be right? To feel right is to be angry.

So, we're just mapping our way through this terrain of Consciousness, right now. We're moving through it. We don't care where we end up.

*The Sun of Being, May 29, 2004, DVD #8*

## Supreme Consciousness Is so Intimate That It Denies the Sense of Otherness

There's no way to translate the Silence into language, so it's futile to look for the bridge. You can't tell anybody about the Absolute Reality. You can't turn it into a subject or an object, a thing or event, a happening, or even the present moment. All of those are concepts and this is not a concept. The sensation of being alive and awake is not a concept.

What is a concept is everything that you conceive of as happening after that fact has occurred. After the fact of living, everything is a concept. And that Supreme Reality is always in movement, so you can't focus in on it and talk about it. You can't look at it, locate it, and then describe it. It doesn't move that way. You can only do that to something that's dead. This thing is living. It's constantly alive in its own dimension. It survives as its own intensity. You can't translate it into another intensity. You can't break it down into the field of understanding.

There's a different way to approach it, to feel it, to know it—a different way. You could say a wayward way, a way that does not engage in linearity, in linear thinking or linear consciousness. It's a great mystery how, once it's realized, it protects itself from you. It protects itself from the scrutinizing mind. If it didn't protect itself, cloak itself, separate itself out from the finite functioning of the human being, it would be destroyed.

The Supreme Consciousness won't let itself be fiddled with. It will not allow itself to be analyzed or tampered with in any way. So, that's a great mystery, how that infinite, pure,

Radiant Being only radiates out of itself and does not let anything else into itself. Isn't that beautiful? Just think of that, what kind of thing that must be, that does not allow for anything to enter into it, touch it. Yet, it's freely exposed. It's unenclosed. It's open and free and yet you can't go near it. You can't approach it, not because of fear, not because it's afraid, but because it's so intimate that it denies the sense of otherness.

This is almost something like a Mobius strip we're talking about here, or like the infinity symbol. It's so radically open that the slightest sense of differentiated consciousness causes it to disappear, even though it neither appears nor disappears. There are certain things you're not allowed to peek at. When you peek at them, they go away like magic. If you understand the way magic occurs, it's not magic any more. It's only magic insofar as you are innocent, in an innocent state of awareness—to just accept "what is," to just accept what's happening. This, too, this Supremely Awakened State, is like magic—it is Magic.

*Organic Functioning, December 14, 2004, DVD #18*

# You Learn to Be Dependent on an Energy Source, Which Is Everywhere

Part of the process of growth is to become disillusioned within the process of growing, to feel despair in the process of growth, to feel like you failed in the process of that evolution. So, if you think this is all about success and attainment, you're wrong. If you think it's only about Light and Illumination, you're wrong.

Within the context of waking up, it's about falling to your knees in helplessness, not the traditional kind of helplessness described in religion and religious literature, where you start praying to a deity. It's not that. It's that you become absolutely "fallen"—you fall completely and you learn to be dependent on an Energy Source, which is everywhere, as opposed to the limited kind of willful energy that is generated in a deluded individual—an ignorant individual who thinks all of their energy is self-willed, who thinks that they do it all.

So, the recognition that Consciousness is everywhere, is the quintessential recognition that "you are That." Then, naturally you begin to project all your actions and all your desires from that Field without thinking about it, without doing it as a technique and without thinking that you've been saved, even by the recognition of the completeness of what I'm talking about.

So, in the end, you haven't gained or lost a single thing. You simply have to work your process until it's over. You have to see it through to the end. That's the only way you get to the end of it. There's no skipping anything. You are the raw material upon which this thing is happening.

Great help will be given here. You're interfacing directly with the wholeness of Consciousness in this instance with me.

So you are going to be jolted into a new level. It's going to shake up whatever you have become stabilized in and continue this process. When I say you get to the end, that's kind of "iffy." I'm using language dangerously, perhaps a little carelessly. There is no end. Evolution just continues. After your own fulfillment has occurred, then you simply witness through your own life the further evolution of everything around you.

In some sense, you are directly connected now to everything's evolution. So, this whole idea that you're just a limited individual and you're small, that dissolves. You're identified completely with the world, completely with the entirety of the world. You are the world.

You don't think small, except when you have a meal and you prefer this over that, or you have this kind of tea over that kind. But, there's no smallness in terms of psychological reality. Your own psyche is permeating nature as a whole.

You'll begin to feel this hugeness that I'm talking about now. But, don't become conditioned by the loss of your suffering. Still nevertheless, this is such a remarkable thing that when what is prior to attention asserts itself, and dissolves that roughness we call suffering, that should be noted. That should be recognized.

*Satisfaction Desire Recognition, March 1, 2009, DVD #34*

Why were you born? Why did you take this body? To realize that you're the whole universe, that's why.

part [3]

# Kundalini-Shakti

## Golden Star

In my Self
you shine like a golden star,

alone and untouched
among the thousand silver ones,

never to be known,
only felt,

in the deepest recess of Being.


[1978]

# The Realizer Is a Walking Vehicle of Cosmic Shakti

Depending on the circumstances of an Avatar's birth, that final stateless-state might have a very powerful transmission capability. He may act as a relay point, as a transmitter for all kinds of subtle spiritual energies. Even though his own evolution is over, it's as if he moderates the functioning of the collective consciousness.

He or she acts as a facilitator for the evolution of those who have not passed through the various states of transcendence, the samadhis or satoris. So his very presence, or her very presence, acts as an ignition-flame, a flame of great conscious intensity, one that you could say is always burning in its own depths. It's always churning in its own region of invisible transparency. As he or she lives life, it's a display of that invisible power that life communicates spontaneously. It's the very texture of Being itself, based on the person's vasanas at the time of birth.

By vasanas, I mean the tendencies that the person was born with. He or she can become an incredible display of spiritual power in the relative field, in the relaxed condition of sahaja samadhi, where there's no use for anyone or anything, in the sense of utilitarian consciousness. It's as if you're sitting by the ocean and you hear these pounding waves, the power of it, but that's just what the ocean does. There is really nothing extraordinary about that. It's just a conjunction of wind, water, and waves moving and they pound onto the shore.

When you get to the ocean and you sit in front of those

waves, you feel that something happens in the midst of that organic display. That the pounding, the sound of water on the turf, the sand carrying that huge, deep vibration, radiates something into the human being and creates a particular experience of itself. In the same way, as Consciousness is moving in and through this individual, depending on the circumstances of his birth, it could become a massive display of spiritual power.

He or she can be said to be a walking vehicle of Cosmic Shakti. In fact, she can then provoke the experience of meditation in others, not just radiate it, but also even aggressively provoke it. Of course, there is no violence in that of any sort, just as there is no violence in the ocean when you go to the shore and you hear the intensity of those waves—of course, you don't want to get too close! But, if you maintain a safe and sane distance, you can gather something in that watery power in the same way as when you sit with an individual who is radiating Consciousness. There is a great Energy about their Being that can be sensed, absorbed.

And, for those who are still on a spiritual path, that Energy itself becomes the deliverer, the means of being delivered into the same state as the one who's radiating it—as the teacher, if you call him a teacher. He may just be a spiritual friend. That might be the best term to apply to such a person—a spiritual friend, just a spiritual facilitator.

*Self-Realization and Awakening, May 7, 2005, DVD #7*

# Kundalini-Shakti Is Connected to the Consciousness of Everything

Prana-Shakti, often termed Kundalini-Shakti, is a potent vibratory current, which serves as an initiation mechanism. It utilizes energy to communicate the essence of the Total Divine, which includes Non-Duality or Light, Devotional Intoxication or Love, and raw Spiritual Current. Within the stream of the Prana-Shakti exists a self-sufficient river towards Divine Communion. Kundalini-Shakti is not merely some kind of occult energy. It's been widely misunderstood, unfortunately.

Those who are prejudicial toward the Kundalini-Shakti tend to favor a non-active Absolute. But those who want to enjoy the motion of life and realize the essence of life simultaneously, will often traverse the path of the Prana-Shakti. Energy is just as potent a communicator as is Silence, the silence of the Atman, the silence of Brahman. Silence can very easily turn itself into Current. This is what the ancient mythology of Shiva and Shakti refers to, the marriage or conjoining of Silence—Absolute Stillness—and ascending, descending, all-permeating Current, Current which actually transforms itself into the Living Bliss of the Divine.

Therefore, Kundalini-Shakti should not be seen as an isolated event. It's connected to the entirety of Consciousness and even further, the consciousness of everything. Kundalini-Shakti is also not a unique human event. It's the flight of a bird, the buzzing of a bee, the shades of light off the face of the moon. It's the laughter in a human being and the tears. It's the opening and closing of the eyes. It's sex, the power of sex, of sexual love. It's all of that and more.

*Discussions on the Kundalini-Shakti, October 5, 2010, DVD #32*

# Get Your Body to Start Feeling Happiness along Side This Awakening Process

*Participant:* Some people experience Kundalini and are awakened, are thrown into infinite Bliss and other people experience Kundalini awakening and they're thrown into infinite pain.

*David:* Right.

*Participant:* How do you respond to the people who are in deep pain? What do you offer to them? What is your own feeling about why that happens, why some people get the Bliss and other people don't?

*David:* Most people just get the Bliss around me, believe it or not. Most people just get the Bliss, with a few exceptions here and there, with the exception of baggage they bring in that might need to be scrutinized by the immense power of Consciousness. When you're talking about Kundalini, you're talking about the immense power of the universe, so you cannot casually walk into that and expect to be stable. One definition of casualness is that not a lot of meditation may have happened before encountering Kundalini. There may not have been a transition period available with which to acclimate the nervous system to that immense energy. So, theoretically, people can go haywire, not just theoretically, but actually.

When people write to me on the Internet asking about what to do, I say, "Come to see me if you can. Just get into communion with me, spiritual communion, so that I can open up more avenues for that Current to flow in and at a greater rate, so we culminate this thing and get it over with." If you catch on fire, you don't want to just walk for a few blocks before you put it out. You would rather incinerate or put it out quickly. It's best that they simply bring the process to fulfillment with the proper spiritual guidance.

Things like eating right food should be stressed, eating good, wholesome, nutritious, sattvic foods, staying away from adrenaline-peaking substances, like sugar and a lot of caffeine. Also, taking those sorts of supplements that can ease and comfort the nervous system, bring nutrition to it and a lot of soothing qualities—even using amino acids and regular vitamins and minerals, herbs, all the things that are available.

Also, exercise is very important. I know you know that because we've discussed this before. But everybody might not understand that your physical body should be as strong as possible. Get out and walk. That's one of the things I would tell people, immediately. Next to good eating, I want you walking for an hour to two hours a day, just walking by yourself and breathing and feeling and opening.

Get yourself so your body is going to start to feel happiness *alongside* that awakening process—so you can begin to *re-discover* your human self *as awakening is occurring*, not wait until the end to find out what this human life is all about. Do it all at once—just do it.

This intensity of the Shakti is actually a blessing. It's the greatest blessing. It's not a calamity. It may feel like a calamity, I agree, and you might go through very upsetting and unnerving times if you're just dealing with Kundalini-Shakti. It's tempered through meditation. It's also tempered through service and devotion. Those things tend to smooth out the process. If you're dealing with just pure, raw energy, you're dealing with a cat with fangs, in the forest, right? Grrrrr. It has one thing in mind and you can't pet it casually.

I like to say on my website that "Love is on the hunt now. Love *is* on the hunt." It's this time in creation where things have gotten so dark spiritually that all kinds of bright tigers come out to help. Fierce, powerful spiritual figures will arise and begin to help, begin to shine their glory right in the midst of this mess.

It's not going to wait around for humans to clean up their act, because they're helpless without this Energy. So the Energy has to come in and do everything. It will pounce upon you. It will come into your life, hopefully easily, hopefully with the Bliss aspect emphasized.

I always tell people, avail yourself of what's available and begin searching. Your body will help you find what you need. You can't just rely on Consciousness to do the whole thing, because there's a real human body that may have to show up to work the next day. You have to pacify that thing. You have to make it happy on its own level. At the same time, the most important thing is to come in contact with a fully Self-Realized Master.

Yet, not many spiritual masters have full realization of the Atman as well as full activation of the Kundalini-Shakti, simultaneously, along with intact Devotional Love—that is, the kind of love that serves and feels each other, which is open-hearted in nature.

*Participant:* But many people are just on their own.

*David:* It's very sad that that is the case, but it's always been that way. Also, you have to look at the spiritual samskaras within that person. They have to get to know themselves and find out why this period of awakening is becoming so difficult. It's going to take a tremendous amount of human effort to let this thing expand and the heart must come into it, the mind must come into it. You don't want to be fully active in Kundalini and be unable to use your rationality, be at the whim of pure energy to display maddening qualities, things that would frighten people. All these things come into play. It's a huge topic, a wonderful topic.

I think Kundalini-Shakti is part of full realization. I don't consider somebody truly realized who does not understand what that is. Yet, men are out there still trying to take control, trying to make the basis of existence That, which is merely transcendental, merely and only That. It's very safe. They spent so much time getting this little realization. You bring in something that is foreign to them and they don't want to rock the boat. They don't want to go through "that" again, because now they're going to have to surrender in terms of energy, the way that they surrendered in terms of meditation. Who's up for that? I am. I am up for it.

*Participant:* Some of us didn't have much choice.

*David:* There should be no choice, ultimately.

*Participant:* I was thinking earlier that the Shakti is always fluctuating from Bliss to Fire, like it hits the samskaras, or whatever it is that's in there. It starts burning through and you feel it. It's like this heat. It's really very, very furious, just like that tiger you were talking about wandering around in the ether. So, it's intense and it will spontaneously melt, or sometimes erupt into Bliss, sometimes a beautiful melting.

*David:* Beautiful. I also tell people it's good to develop a long-term relationship with me. I try to talk to people about the benefit of developing a long-term relationship with me, in my Spiritual Energy, so that the Shakti can be nourished continuously, not just the raw Shakti, but also the Divine Love and the Non-Dual aspects, which are also fully realized here. The Non-Dual acts like a cushion. You won't go mad if you know you're God. No matter how high the Kundalini gets, you'll be in that sacred space of silence. You know that the Kundalini can't burn That. Water cannot wet it. Fire cannot burn it. Wind cannot dry it. You have that conviction established, that "I am That."

Let the Kundalini continue to burn. That way all the circuits get opened up. You don't want to just be dead and realized, like so many are, either half-realized and half-dead, or totally realized and totally dead. It's best to get this whole thing burning into the physical frame, so that you can appreciate that your embodied life is divine.

*Discussions on the Kundalini-Shakti, October 5, 2010, DVD #32*

# Once Activated, the Kundalini Will Bring Your Process to Completion

Kundalini aspirants should always know that once the Kundalini is activated, it will bring the process to completion. It has the inherent intelligence of nature embedded in it, just the way a flower comes to blossom.

The crown will open. The heart will burst open in huge Love-Bliss. This is a natural phenomenon. It may seem disjointed right now, but try to live into it. Don't see it as being something that's attacking you. See it as something that's making love to you. Only, you're not energized enough to embrace it, *yet*. It's something that wants to make love to your total being.

So you've got to be ready for every mudra. You have to be ready to take every posture in Divine Mudra. The Kundalini won't be happy going into some part of you that's inert, so it will start energizing that area. That's what we feel as pain. That part of you is dead. That's why you're feeling aggravation. It's been alienated from the rest of you.

Many people are at war with their own sexualities. How is Kundalini going to find a proper home in that body-mind? You have to be at home with everything about your humanness, love yourself entirely. If you're gay, you should be ecstatic that you're gay. Thank God every day that you're not straight!

You must be happy with who you are. You may have come from a miserable childhood, abusive. You may have a lot of purifying to do because of that—still, be glad. When the

Divine knocks on your door, open up, even if you're not ready, even if you say, "Oh my God, I'm letting something in that's going to be intrusive and fiery." So what? What's better time spent than with communion with that Cosmic Energy? So what if everything gets turned upside down. Just put things in perspective. Why were you born? Why did you take this body? To realize that you're the whole universe, that's why.

So, if it's getting in the way of your job, too bad for your job. Stay with the Kundalini. You see, you can't be half-assed with this, not if you want to go to the end of it. You have to be willing to surrender. You have to surrender all your fears and know that that's the highest teaching. People write to me, "I can't function. I'm losing it." I say, "Relax, you've lost it already. You never had a thing when you came into this birth. Now you're complaining that you're losing everything. Where did you get this idea that you accumulated things like that, in that fashion?"

I love this moment. I love being with you. I love doing this. This is time excellently spent. I relish every second of this. We're creating an enlightened spiritual family here. What better thing could we do?

*Discussions on the Kundalini-Shakti, October 5, 2010, DVD #32*

# The Apparent Origin of the Shakti Depends on Your Point of View

*Participant:* Does the Shakti arise from the nature of Pure Being? Or is it literally transferred from you to me? Or is there some middle ground? I'm not clear here.

*David:* It's all those areas. If there's a "you" who enters into this process and who is capable of noticing and interpreting what happens, and that "you" is in duality, you'll still receive the full transmission of the Shakti, and therefore it will come from me. If you are residing more in the Being aspect, the impersonal Absolute, and you feel energy arising out of That—and you feel the Shakti as tingling currents, swirling, rising, descending, deepening—then it's arising out of your own Being.

The way in which you frame your understanding depends on your temperament. If you are an impersonalist, then you will be reluctant to use devotional language to understand and interpret. You will favor more existential explanations and terms, such as the Absolute. The language of advaita Vedanta is a good example of the impersonal. It's a beautiful language. But so are the devotional languages, which come out of this realization.

Don't become confused on the level of understanding. If something is irking you, and you can't make sense of it, just fall back into your experience and the experience will give you the right understanding. Remember, the mind is just a measuring device. It's not going to give you any grand illumination about anything. It's just a tool to distinguish. In this case, in this moment, it distinguishes between the Absolute Being and the relative changing world. That's its highest function. Later on, Consciousness will expand to such a degree it will swallow the whole external world and then you will really know who you are.

*Participant:* This Blissful Energy feels like plugging into a circuit.

*David:* That's the Shakti, very clearly described. That's one aspect of this great field of Spiritual Transmission. Others will feel the great depth of silence, where even thinking a thought becomes impossible. They will be drawn into a profound samadhi, a deep meditation on Being. That's a Non-Dual Transmission. Others will feel nothing but love, overcome by the feeling of Devotion. That's the Transmission of Rapture, Divine Love and Ecstasy. It's a big event we're describing here.

*Talks and Dialog on the Internet, Volume 1, May 29, 2008, DVD #I-1*

# We Have to Deconstruct the Lies of Religion

*Participant:* You know, I grew up in the era when it was very fashionable to be depressed. I was an English teacher and somebody said isolation is not a theme. It is the condition of modern literature and that's true. If you weren't sad, if you weren't depressed, you were superficial, you hadn't really thought about things. So, it was quite a revelation to me that I didn't have to be depressed anymore, that we don't have to live in a wasteland. The Shakti gives people who are very skeptical a way to believe in God, because you no longer have to think God. You can feel God.

*David:* You've got it. Of course, the whole question of religion comes up and this also needs to be re-oriented back toward its root understanding: it is a natural, nature-based event. I'm not interested in having religions affirm that it's their God that's giving the Kundalini—no good. We have to deconstruct the lies of religion at the same time that we affirm this as an organic event. Otherwise, it's going to be the same thing all over again: "my Shakti is going to punch your Shakti in the mouth." We're going to have bully Gods fighting each other, but now in the feminine form. We've got to get out of this idea that the head can interpret fully what is going on. We've got to get out of this idea that the head can interpret fully what's going on in the Heart.

It's a mind-blower that Life itself is Divine. It's Life itself that is God. It's not that God started life. It's not that God is at the end of life, or watches over it. It's that God *is* Life. The Divine is Living. That itself is a Shakti-informed understanding.

*Discussions on the Kundalini-Shakti, October 5, 2010, DVD #32*

# The Entire Manifest Universe Is Due to the Play of the Prana-Kundalini-Shakti

The entire manifest universe is due to the play of the Kundalini-Shakti, Prana-Kundalini-Shakti, the energy that is within the Prana, the Light—the breath of the Universal Consciousness. You could say that it's a Fire that burns within Emptiness. That's a simplified version.

That which gives birth to a star is the same energy that thrills an eagle into flight. It's the same, exact movement. There is only one movement of energy happening and it's an energy that is both controlled and out-of-control. In other words, it has a systematic method or process of enfoldment and you can see that mirrored in organic life as developmental sequences. Apples grow on apple trees. They don't grow on peach trees one year and cherry trees another year. There is a kind of consistency within pattern that shows us that energy will tend to take the same organismic channel with regards to its dharma—the dharma that's inherent within that form. Flowers produce buds and fragrance. Fruit trees produce fruit and flowers. Animals produce offspring.

What is the flower that exists within the human being? What flower or perfume does it radiate? Is that fragrance any different than the fragrance we see in anything that catapults us into wonder or bliss? Is that, in fact, what this entire display of universal functioning is, nothing but a vast flowering process happening from within a single Being and yet infinitely variegated? An infinite number of forms are occurring within that singleness of Being, that non-divided, non-dual core. So life is not coming from somewhere else.

This planet, this world, this universe is not the by-product of anything outside itself. It's simply happening within a well of Being, out of which it is forced to emerge. It is energetically compelled to emerge, and then return, in circular fashion. That whole process of Energy arising out of Nothingness, entering form, outshining form, and then returning back to Emptiness, is initiation into the Kundalini-Shakti in the human context. So, it's natural that we initiate each other, that we are Gods to each other, and function in that way.

Imagine, all these centuries, these thousands of years, animals and organismic lives have been trashed by religion.

Please, just contemplate that for a moment. Instead of inviting human beings to see that they are simply unfolding in this gigantic mystery, along with everything else, religion has tried to put human beings on a pedestal, convincing them that they are actually superior to the whole show—that they're the main actors and actresses, redeemed by other "special" human beings, who are called saviors, gods.

If we were to admit that everything is sacred, we'd have full responsibility for loving everything, and that appears to be too much for the human being. So it takes the easy way out. It self-exalts with illusory concepts and self-grandiosity, pride and arrogance. It self-exalts and then looks down upon the rest of the world.

This Energy that I'm sharing with you, along with the correct understanding of what it is, will produce a radically opposite conclusion: that the entire world is sacred. There is no stepping out of the sacred and, in this way, I'd like to propose to you the notion that we are meant to endlessly initiate each other out of the Consciousness and Energy that is in the very fabric of life. That's the real purpose of existence, to come to that level of development. So, your body-mind is as sacred as a star forming out of space. It has all of the same potentiality in it and the Kundalini-Shakti, absorbed and meditated upon with great fervor, devotion, and sincerity, will actually begin to educate you in that way. But, it's from *within* life that we will see our exaltation, not from a perspective outside of it.

So, you can see that the kind of understanding that we are heading toward with this kind of teaching is completely, 180 degrees away from anything we've been taught in religion. There is no language for this, because the human being has not evolved enough to appreciate this. Only a few cases here and there have tasted this kind of experience and have shared it with humanity. But, the time is coming now when this Energy is running rampant. It's looking to house itself in as many nervous systems as possible. So, do you have a "for rent" sign on your nervous system, "for lease," or "occupancy available?"

The key is to become initiated. I can't stress this enough. Initiation is simply confronting that Radical Force within your own life, within your own body-mind, and watching the way it functions, the way you begin to function when it enters into you.

I hope this is real for you. I hope I'm not just up here giving a talk. I hope you're touching this Sacred Energy, that it is undergoing initiatory prowess in you as it strikes the different organs in your body, as it strikes your brain, as it strikes your eyes and your mouth.

Once the process of initiation gets going, it will turn into Light. That Energy will turn into Light, the Light of Consciousness.

We take steps very slowly here, just one step at a time. By the time this Energy flowers, there may not be any world for you to deal with. So, when we try to understand this from our human point of view, as a series of sequential steps in the development of consciousness, we do so at our own peril, because we really don't know what this is going to flower into. You're going to be quite shocked when the whole thing begins to really make itself known to you. You're going to be in utter, transcendental bewilderment.

But don't worry about the world. In the meantime, just do the best you can. Use your intelligence, the good mind that was given to you. Use that mind to adapt with this growing consciousness that's happening within you now—and have confidence in yourself. Don't think lowly of yourself. Always think highly of yourself. Think: "I am the Full Consciousness." Marry yourself to that declaration, that "I am That. I am the Absolute. There's nothing higher than my own Self." Once you adopt that view, then these experiences tend to find their way toward stabilization, because you've given them a huge area with which to adapt. But, if you have something of a smaller understanding and you start to get these experiences, then the experiences don't integrate that well with the understanding of the mind.

We're going to do everything tonight. We're going to do it very slowly and we're going to get the Prana-Shakti going to such an extreme that everything will become Non-Dual.

It just goes at its own pace. I'm not the author of this. I'm simply a mouthpiece, that's all. I'm not "more special" than anybody in this room. That has made itself known to me, and through me, I hope that it becomes known to you.

I don't know exactly how that occurs. We call it Diksha. We call it Darshan. We call it the process of Yoga. We call it Kundalini-Shakti. We have many names for it, but the names are just labels. As you know, if you have entered into this process, it's label-less. It's just your life becoming accentuated and intensified from within. So, you may not necessarily understand more, but you will become more. You will become it, within. You have to be both restless and very patient at the same time. You have to always be asking for more, but very happy where you are.

Blossom in your relaxation, not from your restlessness. That's why it's so important to just be where you are, because then it comes up right through that. And so, you were who you were, and in that you have something that is neither added to yourself nor subtracted. It's just an illumination and you can deal with it nicely.

We're just relaxing with each other, like old friends, just coming and being together. But, we do it with a very special kind of Energy that's present. We want to really get that going, get it nice and deep and thick, so that our attention becomes radicalized. We'll inhabit a radicalization of Consciousness.

So, we start off humble, but then it gets like Mount Everest before you know what's happened. Come into your Heart. Forget about your head. We're going to leave the head behind. We're about to take a turn. We're going about 90 mph, making a quick turn, so if you're not in the Heart, you'll miss it. You'll miss the thrill and terror of that turn.

*Prana-Kundalini-Shakti, Autumn 2009, DVD #26*

# If You Experience the Shakti, You're Shaking the Hand of God

If you experience the Shakti, you're shaking the hand of God. You shouldn't worry about anything after that. You don't need to keep on experiencing it "over and over" again. Once you have the full force of the feminine aspect of Being hit you, you've shaken hands with God. That's it. It's going to continue to guide your life, whether you experience it again or not.

Just as, if you've dipped into the silence of No-being, of Non-being, if you've touched that, you've dissolved into the Absolute. It means that you can't undo that. You've seen it. If you've seen it, it's going to keep coming back to you in some form. You're going to be re-led back to that condition. In other words, the evolutionary process will take over after you have had an initial awakening, whether it's in the form of the Shakti, or whether it's in the form of glimpsing No-self.

*An Evening of Dialog, October 8, 2009, DVD #25*

# What We Are Looking for Is the Marriage of Shiva and Shakti

*Orley:* A comment from a viewer in Israel: "When the mind is in rest the Energy penetrates it immediately."

*David:* Yes, that rest is very important, because Shakti is like a magnet to that restfulness, to that restful silence. Shakti will emerge out of empty Shiva, quiet Shiva, relaxed Shiva. So, what we're looking for is the marriage of Shiva and Shakti. We want to feel how they interpenetrate. We want to feel our own Being making love to itself, which is the highest form of tantra. It's what all tantra points to: the inner alchemical transformation whereby the Energy within your own Being makes love to itself. Yes, you can still have an outer lover. I know what some of you are thinking. Yes, you can still have a person. It does not compete with worldly life.

Breathe into this Energy, breathe into it. It's okay to breathe.

As that Kundalini hits your vital area, it is naturally drawn up the body-mind and through the head. When it hits the head, you are issued into Undifferentiated Consciousness.

It's a sensual voyage to the Non-Dual, whereby through energy, through the intensification of energy and the stimulation of the entire chakra system, in a very easy way, you can feel how the Self is produced out of that Energy.

You'll notice, after you leave my program, perhaps in the past you've noticed this, when we've been saturated with Divine Energy for a long period of time; that when you step outside you feel very big. You feel enormous. That's the Non-Dual having given birth through that channel of Kundalini.

*Prana-Kundalini-Shakti, Autumn 2009, DVD #26*


# The Shakti Knows Exactly What to Do

*Participant:* When I do the meditation, I experience the Shakti.

*David:* Yes.

*Participant:* And it basically goes in spirals.

*David:* Yes.

*Participant:* And it knows exactly where to go to remove the blockages.

*David:* I should hope so. It created the whole universe.

*Participant:* Yeah.

*David:* It knows exactly what to do. It's quite smart.

*Participant:* So, it does remove the blockages?

*David:* Absolutely. Sometimes it goes around the blockages. I mean, the nervous system itself as form is a block, so you've got to begin to dwell within the Energy and turn your attention into the Energy. You'll still be a form. So, let the Energy do everything for you. This is the initiation. This is Initiation.

*Participant:* And the truth becomes intense. It's not *just* what you feel when you're meditating.

*David:* Beautiful. So you can be assured that if it's active, it's purifying all the time. It's like a fire, like a Vedic fire, where you symbolically burn all the obstacles. You burn all the obstructions, right? When they do puja, they're doing it with the help of fire and the fire eradicates all the blockages. So, this is the true Spiritual Fire that you're tasting as Spiral Energy. That's the holy, sacred Kundalini. It's going to do the whole process for you.

*Participant:* And then the fear just stops?

*David:* Yes, it's beautiful.

*Participant:* So, when you said that the Consciousness makes itself known to you, it does it in a very subtle form. But, then there's a doubt.

*David:* Where is the doubt?

*Participant:* Is it the mind playing a trick or is it Consciousness itself?

*David:* It's like being in love. If you thought you were in love, would you sit down and say, "Is that my mind playing a trick" or would you trust it?

*Participant:* Trust it.

*David:* Yes, trust this too. Even if it's a trick, believe it. Beat the mind at its own game. The mind will never, ever believe anything. It will disagree with everything. If you tell it, "You are the Infinite," the mind will say, "No, I'm not." If you say, "You are Kundalini-Shakti," the mind will say, "No, I'm not." If you say, "You are Divine Love," the mind will say, "No, I'm not."

So that's the nature of the mind. The mind is always good to help navigate and discern things in life. It helps with the field of duality. It's not so good in the spiritual realm, unless you get to the subtle form of the mind, until you get to the fine intellect, you get to bindu. Do you know what bindu means? It's the finest tip of the intellect. That's a good place, because beyond that is Pure Consciousness.

Don't worry so much. If you're having a good experience, then you must believe it. Otherwise, where would these tears come from? I mean, you can't fake that, right? So, those tears are confessing something. They're telling you that you know with your heart.

*Prana-Kundalini-Shakti, Autumn 2009, DVD #26*

# Let Your Solar Plexus Open Up, Let This Love Power Strike You Here

Let your solar plexus open up. Don't block, just relax there. Relax in your pelvis and your solar plexus. When you get hurt too much, what happens is that this area develops a continual knee jerk reaction to protect. You don't want to let anything in because you think, "I can't deal with one more blow in my vulnerable areas." So then what arises is a reflexive action to keep shutting this down, so nobody hurts you.

Here, it's just the opposite. It's happening now. It's almost like a flower is coming and blooming right inside that area. Because this is a safe place, a safe atmosphere, a spiritual atmosphere, a nourishing atmosphere, a healing atmosphere, you can let it come open again, let it blossom, that flower in there. There's a big flower, huge flower, many petals, right in back of your belly button, down into your pelvis, into your belly.

You just let that feel happy and warm and comfortable and it will have a huge impact on your mind. And you'll begin to relax that knee jerk reaction, to keep on shutting protecting, guarding, guarding, holding, restricting your breathing.

What's going to help you is to relax in those moments of privacy and communal gathering in the Divine. Let it happen there, where everyone does it together. Everyone is respecting each other's privacy and letting that area heal and wash over with this beautiful energy. You can sense that there's no harm in it, that there's no harm in this room.

That's what allows you to overcome that paranoid response toward shutting down, turning away.

Let this Love-Power strike you here. This is may be one of the only places you'll be able to get it in this form. So let it do its work on you here and see if it carries forth into the rest of your existence, even structuring a kind of protection from these negative experiences that can happen. Maybe you'll be created in a kind of cocoon of Energy and Love that will go with you, that will not let anything harm you.

Create your spiritual practice at home, whatever it is. Create a spiritual practice in the sanctuary of your own privacy.

In dark times, teachings like this arise because of the density of the negativity. It will jump start you, it will go right inside you and get everything activated. All your chakras instantly activated because of the nature of the times.

Teachings like this are reserved for Kali yuga. It's a Kali teaching, a teaching from Kalika, Maha-Kali. These deities represent not some quiet spiritual practice. They represent just going in and making changes at their whim—powerful, visceral, connective, with no inhibition—no "may I, please?" No, it just goes in and changes things, because that's the nature of the times. The times are very dense with ignorance and fear. So this teaching will take birth right away.

It's very powerful in here now; very, very powerful—wide open now.

*Love, Growth And Evolution, March 4, 2011, DVD #35*

# We Could Call It Compulsory Joy

*Participant:* Can you talk about the relationship between Shakti and embodiment?

*David:* [smiling] It's a good relationship. Shakti and embodiment; embodiment is Shakti. That's what gives rise to this area we call the world, where embodiment takes place. All that is on the basis of an invisible Energy humming and stirring in the depths of Being, identical to that Being, necessary for the coming forth of things, processes, events, happenings, relationships.

Shakti is all about embodiment and embodiment is all about relationship. Only in the quiet area of the Absolute do you transcend relationship, in deep meditation, or in apprehension of Nothingness, of Non-Duality. Other than those two exceptions, spiritual realizations need to happen in an embodied form. The embodied aspect is very important as is the Non-Dual.

Remember, Shakti is just that empty quality of Nothingness turned inside-out into Pure Energy, the energy which gives rise to manifestation. It's not any different than that which transcends it. But, it's necessary for the Absolute to transform itself into this energetic aspect for both embodiment and relationship to happen.

It's really one event. It's not as if there are two events going on. It's one simultaneous clap of thunder. It's one shaft of lightning, too quick to be seen with the eye. And yet, that process of manifestation happens over hundreds of thousands and millions and billions of years. It elongates itself through time, so that it can happen slowly and gradually, painstakingly, revealing itself to itself.

Manifestation is all about the Self, revealing itself to itself. But to do that it needs beings. It can't do that without having beings involved and that's what this whole creation is right from the very beginning, if you can talk about a beginning.

The reason why we were designed in embodiment was so that we could taste the ecstasy of living. We could call it compulsory joy. Buddhists, of course, have a hard time with this. For them, relativity is a bad trip. It's a bum trip, because they look at it from the standpoint of loss, not what's gained, not the affluence that produces manifestation, the super-abundance within Being that gave birth to everything. They just look at that narrow area where everything is passing into its dissolution phase, going toward death. That tints their view to such an extreme degree that they're not interested in anything else. They're interested in ending the cycle of rebirth and this impulse has a certain amount of intelligence built into it. There is a stroke of intelligence in that.

*Participant:* Well, I think that philosophy comes from people's experience of pure pain. You're talking about this experience of joy. But if your experience of relativity is all pain....

*David:* That's why I said there's a stroke of intelligence in it.

*Participant:* Right. If I'm going to make a leap, I'd rather tune into the abundance.

*David:* You can't, but Being can bless you in such a way, through Divine-Intoxication, that you begin to sense the joy.

*Shakti, Embodiment and Non-Duality, September 17, 2010, DVD #32*

92

[2007]

[2012]

[2006]

part [4]

Devotion

Joshua Tree National Park

# The Only True Companions You Have on the Spiritual Path Are Love, Trust, and Innocence

The only true companions you have on the spiritual path are love, trust, and innocence. Everything else will betray you. Even the visions, the satoris, the transcendental awakenings, the high devotional experiences, all of these things will come and go. The essential nature of your Self is innocent, without knowledge, without time. That means that the awakened condition is already awakened.

I often say, this teaching is not a guru-based teaching. It is not the sadhana of a yogi that is taught here. In fact, there is no sadhana other than to simply come as you are and to feel and be in your innocence, what you are. That's where this work is done, in the innocence of the Heart.

When you come here, just sit and listen. Be open to your feeling nature. See what passes through you and comes before your eyes. See what floats up from within your heart—just see and feel. Be innocent, open. Don't resist anything.

*The Beauty of Innocence, April 22, 2003, DVD #W-2*

# Just Spending a Little Time Together without Any Motive

When I drop out of the field of speech, does it really matter? It's an effort for me to keep this up. On the one hand, I'm falling like a pail or a bucket down into the well, and gravity is driving this bucket down toward this water. On the other hand, there's a feeling like, hmm, there may be something to say.

You see, when I say I have no teaching, this is what I mean: there's nothing for me to talk about. I have no ideals to propagate. I have no approach to share. It's just spending a little time together without any motive.

It's difficult for some who may come in craving a teaching or craving a particular expression. It could be very difficult to sit, waiting and yearning for something. That kind of approach is just wanting to be stimulated. You want someone to keep on entertaining the active mind.

Whereas, what's happening here, is that we freely move forth between that non-cognitive state of Being and thinking, of experience. Do you see what I mean?

We'll find each other somehow. We'll meet each other. It doesn't have to be forced.

*Inwardness and Beyond, May 13, 2003, DVD #W-3*

# The Primal Hunger of the Human Being, to Love and Be Loved in a Condition of Light

The core of Nothingness in the deepest level of human subjectivity is actually Light. When your eyes become accustomed to that inner darkness, you may actually flash upon Light as being the inmost core of your being. It's literally shining, and when that same impulse begins to look out into the external world, it seeks for love.

Are you wondering why you are all addicted to relationship? It's because that craving wants to meet its final resting place in the external world, not merely to turn back upon an individual's subjectivity, but to actually leap out into what seems to be objective creation and to find a kind of union there: the union of Shiva, or Nothingness, and Shakti, Energy-Bliss-Delight.

They are not two. It's not like one happens and then you wait and then the other happens. This is the hunger, the primal hunger of the human being, to love and be loved in a condition of Light.

*The Field of Feeling, July 2, 2002, DVD #7*

# The Field of Feeling *Is* the Mother

The body, the physical body, is reverberating in that Enlightened Wholeness. It's to be seen, not understood. It's to be felt, not to be known.

If anything allows you to navigate in this external world in the form of the Beloved, in the essence of the Beloved, it's this field of Feeling. It's this Feeling-Vision that leads you around and takes you here or there. It creates your cravings. It creates the satisfaction of your cravings. It will never abandon you.

That is the Mother, the Mother as she is born out of the Un-manifested Being of Pure Consciousness. She finds her way up the human nervous system and then, through that human nervous system, begins to fulfill its desires in a state of exhilarated Light-Apprehension.

No one has a map of this process other than going through it. You will be given a map as you continue on this journey. When you really need it most, a new direction will come up for you, a new desire will emerge. A new lead will be given toward the satisfaction of your desires and the desires of everything simultaneously. And when your desires are taken into account in such a profound way, then all the desires of everything are satisfied.

*The Field of Feeling, July 2, 2002, DVD #7*

# If Your Devotional Posture toward a Realized Being Is Tactful, Intelligent, and Targeted Correctly, Something Like an Omniscient Relationship Can Arise

There are two types of sadhana. There is intentional, deliberate sadhana. Then there is the burning desire for enlightenment. If you practice the former for hundreds of years, nothing will happen, until you have the latter. Somehow, that hunger, that burning, must be awakened within the practice (if you are performing a practice).

When your time comes, if the desire for realization is awakened in its fullness, you won't need any practice. You might take some on, but it's hard to say. It's not something you can know about in advance. So, don't ask me, "Will I need a practice?" I have no idea. That's my "hands-off" approach to your life. I also know to never meddle in someone's spiritual affairs. People come and they say: "I feel so close to realization. Does that mean I can give up my practice?" How do I know?

You've got to be your own teacher in this sense. There's no authority that can tell you. It doesn't matter how highly realized the authority is. They could be the greatest Avatar the planet has ever seen. Yet, they don't know anything about your sadhana, because there is this buffer zone of free will and independence in the field of action that has to surround every human life.

At the same time, if your devotional posture toward a Realized Being is tactful, intelligent, and targeted correctly, something like an omniscient relationship can arise.

So, why is that? I have no idea. I just know it's true.

*Enlightenment Is Not for the "Me," July, 3, 2009, DVD #26*

# This Is a Precious Moment for Me, to Dwell upon You as the Supreme Consciousness

It's a very unique individual who will give his whole life to seeing the Divine in all its forms and become its willing experiment in this birth.

One lives a very semi-transparent existence in this highly awakened condition. One has this sense of living very close to death every second—yet, *meeting* the unknown, the invisible, that which is totally transparent, that which is so near to you that it's your life.

If you don't have that kind of passion and friendliness toward this unnameableness, toward that which is transcending you completely—that *is* you—then you can't proceed completely on the spiritual path. At some point this may all make sense to you, if it doesn't make sense today. There's a fullness of worldly experience and the fullness of meditative experience that combine together into the fullness, the wholeness of the Awakened Heart Consciousness.

One will pass through many forms of samadhi, of temporary awakenings, and then even pass through permanent samadhi, permanent nirvakalpa samadhi, which is continuous awareness of the Divine Consciousness, twenty-four hours a day.

It may not sound logical to say that there is anything beyond that and it's true. There is nothing logically beyond that. What follows that condition of full awakening, of ever-present samadhi, is the realm of Awakened-Feeling.

It's as if you've been a bi-ped your whole life, walking on two legs, and then all of a sudden, you look down and there's a wheel. So, you're given a whole different mechanism with which to proceed, a whole different way of living in feeling now. And, in the end, it's Feeling that survives everything. It's not mere Emptiness.

The fullest flowering is this expressive, invisible Feeling-ness. It's a Feeling that is in samadhi. Feeling *is* samadhi. But it's not a samadhi which excludes external reality, or others, or things. I'm also fond of calling it the Divine Mother Consciousness, Devi Consciousness, the Awakened Feminine. Those terms capture the sweetness, the amrita that is inherent in such a state, the nectarous quality of *amrita sahaja samadhi*, that all-time natural state of being one with the Divine, but added onto it this nectarous Feeling-Bliss.

So, one will never look to isolate in Light again, to dwell on only the Self, or merely in the Self. Such an awakening of pure Self-Realization is profound—it's not to be minimized, but it's also not to be lauded as the highest state. The highest state is not a state. It does not put one on a platform above others. But, if you've been chewing on a peach stone and I offer you a strawberry, I'd be doing you a favor. If you got used to the hard texture of a peach stone, gnawing at that, then I would be loving you by offering you a strawberry, not demeaning you because you had been eating peach stones. So, to chew on the knowledge of the Absolute is to chew on stones. You know what would happen to your teeth. They'll reflect in their image the brittle condition, the actual reality that you express in that state of cosmic isolation of Self-Realization.

This is a precious moment for me to dwell upon you as the Supreme Consciousness, to dwell upon you, which leads to indwelling, indwellingness. You dwell on me. I dwell on you. That dwells on itself. It's unmistakable that that Non-Dual Consciousness is present here. And, then, there is this other quality. For lack of a better term we can call it feeling, Enlivened Feeling.

One can actually feel this substance being produced in the nervous system, this nectar. It almost feels like it's being churned from the innermost recesses in Consciousness. There is this churning and then out of that churning there is this spilling and in that spilling there's this intoxication, this natural state of Intoxicated Feeling. So, let us enjoy this delight. Let us be gracious and appreciative of this delight, this exquisite moment, precious and unfathomable.

*Uniqueness, Awakening and Beyond, May 29, 2002, DVD #5*

# The Absolute I Know Is Full of Love-Intensity

*Orley:* A participant comments, "As soon as you spoke about Bhakti and Krishna, it was like a tidal wave of Shakti hit the shore of Being."

*David:* Lovely, beautiful; Krishna means the All-Charming One, so none of us can resist Him. Even if we try, even if we think we're the most steadfast yogi—He walks in and He's so beautiful—we lose it; and we don't mind losing it for that reason. We're not so self-protected, arrogant, and inflated with the Unmanifest that we would seek to avoid such a thing. Anyone who's avoiding Bhakti on that basis, in the name of advaita, is deluded. Anyone who would run away from love, Embodied Love, the manifestation of it, I consider demented.

So don't ever talk to me about a loveless Absolute. I don't want to hear it. The Absolute I know is full of Loving Intensity, full of Kundalini-Shakti, full of every color you can perceive within and beyond these eyes, full of every form, every consciousness. Everything is in it—nothing is not in it.

*An Evening of Dialog, October 9, 2009, DVD #25*

# Desire, Addiction, and the Power of Awakening Itself

The heart of enlightenment is the innocence of not knowing. That's the real source of all consciousness expansion. In fact, all the degrees of expanding consciousness are nothing but some sort of remembrance of the Divine Not-knowingness of the Heart. That Not-knowingness spawns an innocence, an innocence in which the mind can look at "what is," and what it looks at is the whole mechanism of desire.

Desire originates in silence. It grows in silence and it blossoms in silence. So, really, awakening truly is nothing but the knowledge and the feeling of desire. The innocence that I referred to allows desire to flower spontaneously, and therefore reveal itself in both its gross and subtle aspects. In its gross aspect, desire is clinging. It's pleasure. It's pain. In its subtle aspects, desire begins to show itself. It begins to expand in subtlety and unveil its reality as Pure Energy.

When desire is not interfered with, when it's neither rejected nor repressed, it's allowed to show itself. And innocence then is the Divine Fabric upon which desire can communicate its innocent intensity.

Think of a snake coiled. If it's likened to the process of desire in its gross aspect, it simply stays rigidly coiled upon itself. But if it's allowed to expand, if it's allowed to show itself, it will uncoil like a cobra, and it will rise, still in the essential position of coiledness, which is its nature.

So desire rises out of the Silence when it is given safe permission, with a non-judgmental, non-struggling, non-violent mind, a mind that is not addicted to ideologies, teachings, and understandings. Then what one is watching is the actual process of Life itself.

Desire is life. It is the movement of Life-Energy and it only arises totally and unrestrictedly in a subjectivity that is free and unencumbered. Otherwise, like a snake, it will just slither away under some stone, and go down into some hole where it can't be seen.

In its gross aspect desire can become addiction. Desire can become coiled into a self-generating process of relationship with objects, and also with the very sensation of desire itself, and stay as if continuously ricocheted upon itself, unable to leap beyond itself. Addiction is that smothered process of desire that has been forced into a narrow area of expression.

Addiction is the suppression and corralling of the movement of desire. You could think of desire in terms of the use of recreational substances like tobacco and alcohol. What these substances do is suppress desire from actually expressing itself. They keep it bound in a safe circle of continuous self-expression that doesn't really break out of itself. It's a circular movement of desire that's self-contained and self-generating. It's certainly still the energy of life, but it's not allowed to actually set itself free and move into its subtlety.

Can the human being ever be free from the propensity toward addiction and its potentiality? No. Is the Enlightened Person free from addiction and the potentialities contained in addiction? Absolutely not. Someone who is enlightened has simply been released into the total energy of want, of wanting. That is, he or she has found a secret to *potentially* bypass the inherently self-sabotaging nature of gross desire and penetrate into the subtle movement of desire within Consciousness. He or she can feel the circulation of desire moving in the freedom of Consciousness. And while moving in Consciousness with desire, when desire is able to finally have its way, when it's not thwarted into artificial circularities, such as tobacco and liquor addictions, artificial patterns which keep it gross, it can penetrate and break loose the various psychological blocks in the personality.

It's like a fire that's been flamed into intensity, when it's allowed to move in the Heart, in the Transcendental Heart. Otherwise, desire is condemned toward remaining in a very, very small territory of subject/object relations. So we're talking about a kind of implosion of energy into the field of desire, which allows it then to expand or uncoil and reveal its primal longing, its painful longing for simple release.

Desire is a mindless force. It's not some small energy. It's not some conditioned reflex. Desire is the power and process of awakening itself, before and after realization. So, desire is constantly circulating in a Realized Being, but it's been totally released into freedom.

When an Enlightened Being acquires *total* awakening, and the movement of desire has been yielded into the Infinite Silence, and the Infinite Silence willingly releases itself back into the field of desire, and there's no fixed place of abidance any longer, then the Enlightened Being takes on a quality of whatever he beholds or whatever beholds him.

Anyone who sits with an Enlightened Being will soon realize that the Enlightened Being becomes whatever the person perceives him to be. So, if there is a great longing in someone to see total freedom, it's as if, metaphorically, imagistically and energetically, the Enlightened Being becomes an eagle with his wings spanned, floating effortlessly on the winds that keep him buoyant, frictionlessly floating effortlessly in the silence of the Absolute.

Or, if a person craves to see anger in the Enlightened Person, he or she will manifest anger for that person to see, so that that desire can be liberated of what we call negative emotions: rejection, fear, anger, attachment, loathing, indifference. The Enlightened Person will continuously manifest a whole, transcendental tapestry for anyone who needs to see something, and all of that takes place in and for the movement of desire.

There is nothing else in the entire universe except for Desire and Freedom. Everything you see, all the forms, the animals, they are forms of desire. Plants, insects, fish, rocks, clouds, mountains, they are all forms of desire, desire of the Invisible One who is not a person, who is not a thinking entity, and has nothing in him or her that is remotely connected with the human being. That Force, which manifests the whole universe, manifests itself as an infinite spectrum of desire.

And so, each one of us is also manifested out of that desire, the desire of the Absolute to know itself, the desire of the Absolute to come into its own feeling through that organism.

*The Innocence of Not Knowing, October 2, 2004, DVD #12*

## The Spiritual Life Truly Does Not Begin until You Bring Love into the Process

The spiritual process truly does not begin until you bring Love into the process. You can call it Love, Devotion. You can call Love, Surrender. You can call Love a Vast Ocean of Quiet Awareness, of Quiet Consciousness. Whatever you call it, it's a single happening inside the Heart, the Heart Center, and by that I do not mean the heart chakra. I mean the entire center of gravitational feeling that pulls one ever deeply inside of oneself. Love is the recognition of that reality, of that felt force of inward-drawing consciousness and open-hearted surrender to the very nature of Being— recognizing that pristine, shining quality of Pure Awareness—a field that is outside of duality.

Two things—this Love cannot happen except in surrender and its nature is non-dual. We can't speak of Love in the spiritual sense in terms of duality. We can't even have a separate god or godhead that we direct our attention to, in the hope of receiving grace. There must be an immediate deconstruction of this whole idea of separateness and as that occurs there will be this blossoming of Love in the spiritual process. It will become the entire spiritual process and that's how you will know whether you are moving along. You will know because you are flowering in Love and that experience cannot be missed. That experience is so intoxicating, so sweet, so all-pervasive, that you cannot miss it. You can miss almost anything else—knowledge, understanding—but you can't miss the unfolding of Love in the spiritual process. It's like a gigantic explosion happening within your subjectivity.

That Love will dilate you, just the way an eye, its pupil,

will dilate to accommodate more Light. The soul dilates in the presence of that Love, letting in that tremendous area of Consciousness that binds everything together. Such an explosion is incalculable in terms of its effect on consciousness, on the consciousness of an individual. It obliterates that consciousness of separation and therefore it dissolves individuation, the process of evolving individuality. It brings an end to it. Love takes that individuated essence and dissolves it into the Ocean of Nectar.

You will know that has happened when all of your energy arises spontaneously out of that Ocean, when your own individual ego-structure has come apart. It has become dismantled and what has replaced it is an Oceanic Energy, an energy with no beginning or end, and you will begin to live in that. You will begin to extract what you need from that on the most material, or gross level of living and in that flow of Energy and Light and Love there will be a corresponding recognition in the clarity of awareness.

*Love and Light, June 17, 2011, DVD #39*

# I Don't Have a Choice but to Be Profoundly Attracted

*Orley:* A viewer in Australia comments, "Thank you, David. I am drawn into a laser focus by your words. Attention is fixed on the Real and on trust."

*David:* That's what I want. I want you capable of this kind of gesture, a gesture born within Grace. It's a non-accomplished gesture. It's a flowering, not effortfully produced, a sort of samadhi within itself. That's the symptom or the indication of receiving Transmission, receiving Diksha, receiving Darshan. Ultimately, you've got nothing but your life. That's the teaching. It's all within.

*Orley:* Viewer says, "No, nothing to do with me. I don't have a choice."

*David:* That's correct. When you enter into this kind of listening, when you're drawn in that deeply, that innocently, you'll find that you can't even explain how it all happened. You can't even know how you got there, which means, exactly as you said: "There's no choice in this." It's not about choosing. It's not about directing your attention. It's not about engaging in your separateness. It's about presuming something that is prior to that, innocently.

*Orley:* Viewer says, "I don't have a choice, but to be profoundly attracted."

*David:* Good. That's how the Gopis were. They had no choice. Running around crazy, they had no choice but to be attracted. You see, they got Darshan from Krishna's physical form. He wasn't teaching yoga techniques. He wasn't teaching jnana yoga. He wasn't teaching Self-inquiry. He'd walk by and they'd run after him like a bunch of bees running after a jar of honey.

So in that case, when you're talking about attraction and the most attractive condition, you're pointing toward Darshan through the physical body of the Master, in which case you don't even have to invert your attention within your own being. It's flooding you from without. It's a paradoxical Darshan. That's what was sending the Gopis insane. The more they got, the more they wanted. There's something to be said for that kind of insanity. Even the Bliss of the Self will have the same impact upon you, even though it does not necessarily come from the outer body of a Master. It might, but it doesn't necessarily have to. That, too, will send you into a kind of insanity, a Love of something invisible, uncreated.

*An Evening of Dialog, October 9, 2009, DVD #25*

# My Understanding Is Rooted in Innocence

*David:* Nothing is going to be imposed by me from without. You'll never get that. I'm the most anti-authoritarian teacher on the planet, which means all of my understanding is rooted in innocence. I believe that innocence is the foundation of the spiritual process, innocence and that alone, and you were born that way.

*Participant:* As far as the difference between the Father teachings and the Mother teachings, the Father teachings take the nut and try to crack it open. But the Mother teachings bury the nut in the soil and water it, and then it blossoms.

*David:* So, it's non-aggressive is what you're saying.

*Participant:* Right, and it succeeds where hammers and hard things fail. It succeeds with this soft energy of love and dirt.

*David:* So, the dirt is sacred in this teaching.

*Participant:* Yeah. [Laughs]

*Prana-Kundalini-Shakti, Autumn 2009, DVD #26*

# Love Is What Wins in the End

Where do birth and death come from? I don't even know that. How are you going to find out where that little thing comes from? Don't worry about it. You're fiddling with mosquitoes, a blip; just get a net, wear the net.

Just commit to this Love-Moment. I want to be the Love-Offerer, dispensing Grace. Do you want it? It's not from a literal "me." Don't worry, it's just a manner of speaking.

Everyone is looking for this. Even the Enlightened are looking for love, even after they get enlightened. Go tell that to all those "teachers" who have no clue. Love is what wins in the end. And that's why, even after all the great enlightenments we've seen on this planet, from all the Great Beings who've had it, the world goes on in spite of all their "great" awakenings. The world didn't stop existing. Love is what wins in the end.

So the Self, written with a big S, is not superior to the world. The world is superior to the Self because, no matter how deeply realized you get, when you wake up there's still downtown. It's still there. All those stores are on the street. So, they win, not your realization. You have to become humble about this.

When you're Awake and become unconcerned with That, then you're really awake. When you become unconcerned and disinterested towards your own Infinite Bliss, when you don't even care about it, then you're really enlightened. You have no movement toward That, no response toward it. We're talking real freedom here. This is radical freedom, even freedom from Non-Duality.

So, you can get up and make some tea. You can have some nice tea in the morning and enjoy it. You don't have to make excuses anymore for your body-mind, somehow asking forgiveness for being in a body-mind.

You're exactly where you should be. You're exactly in the right world. You're exactly in the right family, no matter how bad it is. Here, you're in my family. I forge a new genetic family. I penetrate your DNA in this room.

Consciousness is talking now, no individual. We're on the crest of a wave now. We're just riding the crest.

*Talks and Dialog on the Internet, Volume 5, July 24, 2009, DVD #I-5*

# This Is Beautiful, This Is Love-Tantra, This Is Real Tantra

It's not enough to just have the Non-Dual. It's good to have the Kundalini come up and begin to awaken all the circuits in the body-mind. It's a distinctly different realization. Non-Dual realization concerns itself with the origin of the mind, with the mind's habitat.

The Kundalini-Shakti we're talking about is a kind of bioelectrical event in nature that swirls into the nervous system, giving it great vitality, bodily ecstasy, an ascending and descending Current of Light, Vibratory Light. It's very crucial to a distinctly different form of awakening, one that isn't strictly non-dual, which will tend to dismiss the world. So, the Kundalini is an invitation to live in the world, awakened.

The Non-Dual aspect will always feel foreign in the world because it doesn't mix with anything. It's one hundred percent Absolute. But the Kundalini-Shakti is not like that. It flows right into the energy of biological organisms. Its root is in the Light, the same Non-Dual Light, but what it does is give gradations of Light-Energy to the body-mind, so that the body-mind can be comfortable in a high state of spiritual delight, and also link the Absolute and the relative.

We humans don't have a clue as to how this life should be lived, how tremendous the Bliss of this birth is. We're so "bad," we even get lost in spiritual teachings! That's how "bad" we are!

I want to take you all on this journey, just by being here with you, not by taking you through practices. I just want to offer this, offer it, that's all. I'm just offering. There's no condition.

So, this is something precious. When you have something precious, you hide it. You never show it off. You don't wear it on your sleeve. You bury it inside your heart. Otherwise, if you bring it into the light of day, you're going to look with those daylight-consciousness eyes, and all you're going to see are fragments, splinters, and more suffering. No matter what you bring out, no matter how beautiful it was within, when you bring it out into daylight-consciousness, daylight-consciousness will get its fangs out. You've got to have this thing about you that understands that certain things are meant to stay in the dark, a secret forever.

You see, this is Divine Love. Forget about the Kundalini. Now we're in the Divine Beloved, the Pure Love aspect. Kundalini itself can go away. Now we have a Light of Love.

It's beautiful, isn't it? This is tantra. Don't wait to do tantra with a man or a woman. You'll never get it. This is beautiful. This is love-tantra. This is real tantra. This is "red" tantra. It's not "white" tantra. This is the same feeling of bodily ecstasy you get in ecstatic lovemaking with another human being.

*Participant:* So grateful.

*David:* Me too, very grateful. We share it. We're all grateful to that Divine Energy. I show up and it comes. I don't know why. It keeps following me. Wherever I go, this tidal wave is lurking just a few feet behind. And then I sit and it's there. It fills a room. That's why I came out and taught. I haven't "attained" anything.

Divine Love can fix any condition, no matter how deep-off-the-end you think you are, or how bad you think your situation is. It can heal almost anything, I've found, no matter what your spiritual dilemma. There are even people who are practically going mad because they're at the end of their sadhana and they don't have the right teacher to help them complete it.

Thank you, all. It's been an ecstatic evening for me and I hope that some of this runs off—like honey—into every part of your being. Namaste.

*Talks and Dialog on the Internet, Volume 5, July 24, 2009, DVD #I-5*

Devotion
is the doorway
to the Heart.

Bliss liberates instantly. The Bliss-Force of Absolute Being dissolves the knot of self-reflexive awareness—the perceiver, the knower, the one who understands and functions in relativity. Egoic consciousness, the "prasad" or leftover of inadequate seeing, is recognized to be an echo within memory's functioning, a subtle auditory hallucination. Ignorance is the crashing of memory-current in the hidden chambers of the mind, the noise that overwhelms the silence. The Master's Heart of Bliss-Consciousness shatters this nagging, self-perpetuating movement and restores the awareness of the Self. There is no room for effort here, only a direct interfacing with the utterly simple, naked and absolute state of Being Itself. Only within and by the Grace of Being can this entire field of self-perpetuating ignorance be renounced, once and for all.

part [5]

# The Master

[2015]

# The Bond with the Master Is a Bridge to Everything

Nature will uphold the path that you're on. Nature will support you. By nature I mean everything, your own inner nature and the nature of the world.

And in this communion with me you're receiving Diksha, you're receiving the Initiation-Power of that fulfilled condition. When realization flowers, a unique fragrance is offered, which stimulates, encourages, and culminates the spiritual evolution of those who are tuning into that Transmission.

Of course, no time limit can be placed on this. We can't say when your process is going to culminate. But you should receive some kind of steady assurance within yourself that the maturation is continuing, deepening, widening, and ultimately disappearing in "what is," in just "what is."

The bond with the Master is a bridge to everything. It's the last relationship you will have. It's the relationship that both fulfills and ends all relationships. Then, you are yielded into the ecstasy of the impossible. You will find your home in a radical condition of impossibility, unreality, something that can't be imagined, a condition that can't be anticipated, formulated, structured, or even understood. You will find a home in that place where knowing stops, goes on stopping, and has stopped forever.

It's very simple, really.

So, be prepared for the most radical. Don't set your sights on something small. Set your sights on everything, until you become everything, until everything becomes you—all beings in your Self and all of the Self in every being. Fix your gaze on That, because if you take your mind off That, you're destined for a lesser state of being. You hold to That and that's where you will go.

So even within the arising of these variously disjointed understandings and incomplete experiences of opening into the Absolute, you learn to stay fixed on your ultimate goal and that's what gets you through. It is your resolution to simply recognize anything less than that Supreme Unity as illusory and undesirable.

*An Evening of Dialog, October 9, 2009, DVD #25*

# Once You've Found a Real, Potent Communicator of the Supreme Reality, Don't Go Anywhere Else

Recognize first that the Spiritual Master is the incarnation of God, all that you call God.

The Spiritual Teacher is the solid bedrock of Transcendental Realization in human form. Having acknowledged him as such, give up all thoughts of going somewhere else. Once you've found a really potent communicator of the Supreme Reality, if you're having ongoing experiences with that Being, I suggest from my perspective of spiritual sanity: don't go anywhere else. Why would you want to dilute that relationship?

Begin to investigate the movement of those energies and

experiences that you have. Trace them back into the Source-Consciousness that you are, and work fervently toward the origin of all spiritual experiences. Let the energy that the Master radiates work through the whole process for you with your loving cooperation and devotion.

Right in this moment, the fire of Reality is activated. It is being communicated. The key is, are you willing, are you able, to make a direct approach within yourself? Are you able to accept that what's happening in this room is you? Yes, I might be instigating it, communicating it, radiating it, but can you own it, too? Can you say "yes" completely into that?

You'll see that there are all kinds of subtle resistances that need to display themselves to your consciousness over time. It may be five minutes, five days, or five years until they exhaust themselves and you come into a sudden acceptance of "what is," you come into total, absolute simplicity, something that I can't describe as a transition for you. It's not able to be described in terms of a transition, from one state of consciousness to another. This final transition is, in fact, the end of states of consciousness. It's waking up from the dream.

The world may have no use for this, but those who are blessed by birth to want and know what this is intuitively—those to whom nature has given itself fully—will understand the greatness of this gift. The world will spit at those who are truly realized in this because it represents a whole new way of being in the world, a way that the world hasn't quite seen yet. If you know anything about human history, about hate based on religion, you know exactly what I'm talking about. You'll understand completely.

There are only a very few who will be attracted into the Radiant Condition, the Radiantly Awakened State, Heart Awakening—only a few people in millions. So, even those odds don't make me feel sad. They make me happy because I know how special it is, that it's inherently esoteric. You can package techniques and you can package teachings, but you can't package the vastness, and why would you want to?

So this is a very unique time to flower, to breathe in the Silence, to breathe in your own Consciousness.

The world is as you are, the future is today, and there is really nothing other than you.

*There's Only You, December 24, 2005, DVD #17*

# The Real Guru Wants to Have an Unrestricted and Infinite Relationship with You in the Self

*Participant:* I see you as the Master and there is love for the Guru. But I sense that love from the Guru is probably much greater. There is a very strong attraction on the level of the soul.

*David:* Well, on the level of your experience, where you feel love for the Master, that love has been given to you by the Master. It's all done by Consciousness. It's all done in the Consciousness of the Master. So, even the love and adoration and devotion you feel, the Guru-relationship that you enjoy, is all given as that ultimate gift. It's all part of the Ultimate Unity.

The Guru just wants to have a relationship with you in Consciousness. The real, true Guru, the real Master, wants to have an unrestricted and infinite relationship with you in the Self, and that's where he makes himself available. That's where he should be most fully present in your experience. The Guru, truly, isn't even relevant until you begin to awaken within your Self, for that's where you find Him.

You never have a relationship with an outer Guru. It's not really that kind of process. You can only have a master-slave relationship with someone who is "other." You can only have a Guru who is an authority figure that would breed that kind of relationship, stressing the outer form of the relationship. But to me, the real Guru is Consciousness itself. It's the Absolute.

And that's where my great desire is, to meet you there, to share that understanding and to taste that reality with you. Even though we both might disappear in the process—we most certainly will and only That will remain—we still enjoy this love for one another en route.

You can feel that sublimity. You can feel how the entire relative mind starts to fall into it. It succumbs. It drops. The whole limited nature of attention falls away and you become ever more immersed in the Consciousness that precedes knowledge and form. It's happening now. It's just happening. It's not happening to "anybody." It's just happening. It's not that "nobody" has to be there for this to happen. It doesn't matter whether there is a "somebody" or a "nobody" there. It's going to happen because it's the truth of this moment.

*Talks and Dialog on the Internet, Volume 1, May 29, 2008, DVD #I-1*

# The Avatar Radiates That Supreme Frequency as If Screaming It through the Whole Bottomless, Fathomless, Apex-less Universe

The human being that is not touching its inwardness hates itself. The human being that is not actually going into its subjective fabric of silent beauty, open heartedness, do-nothingness, is doing the opposite; is accumulating the impressions of experience and becoming enraged by them. As they are collected over time, he builds up more rage because he is not releasing.

So you can grasp intuitively at this point what deep "you know what" we are in, very deep. Yet, at this time in history, other things also begin to happen, because we are still connected to the fabric of nature. The mechanism of nature, in such morbid times, begins to produce very powerful human beings who are born out of the Source-Consciousness.

They are born from within Consciousness itself and they take birth in order to rectify the delusional and psychotic predicament that human beings have created for themselves. The force of their existence, the force of their birth, is enough to begin to realign things, to change the axis of rotation of the earth, to allow for all sorts of subtle influences to be born within the organic condition of Pure Consciousness. These individuals take birth in the Wide-Awake State of Full Enlightenment.

After they take birth, they engage a sadhana so that they can become familiar with the world-consciousness at that time. They deconstruct the accumulated ignorance that they've taken on in their process of human maturation. Then, they throw it off through their spiritual practices. Then they re-remember. They re-cognize their natural state of sahaja samadhi, which is the same state an animal is in except that the context of a human birth gives it a different tone, texture, flavor and power in the ecological makeup of nature. The Avatar radiates the intensity of Shakti with fury, just like a hurricane, a tornado, a blizzard, a rainstorm. On a calm and sunny day, that individual, if you will, begins to radiate a tremendous force of purity, something that surpasses anything imaginable.

It is the most auspicious time for a human being to be born, when such an individual is on the planet. Many thousands and tens of thousands of human lives can rearrange their energy around the presence of that one Enlightened Being, whether they seek him out in person or not. The force of his Transmission will attract people into their own subjectivity, quietly and surreptitiously. Very quietly, mysteriously, people will be led back to the origins of their own existence. As they feed off the Life-Energy, the Bliss-Food, the Life-Consciousness of the Avatar, they will automatically be reset in their direction.

Of course, the real-world scenario is more like a battlefield than a garden. It's here the Avatar just comes and waters everyone and everything. Still, it is more like the Avatar appears on the battlefield of life, as suggested in certain religious texts, and he inhabits and suffers the very friction he's overcoming. He inhabits and endures, overcomes and transcends, and brings others into the transcendence of it. He suffers it with them, suffers it for them, suffers it by them, so that there is a great redeeming power that's revealed in the midst of this psychosis.

It is not any one particular thing that such Beings do that can be considered holy or sacred. Every breath they take is a balm on the suffering body of the planet and the tortured psyches of the people—and not just in this world. Just as there is a gross world here, there are also subtle worlds with beings that have wholly different nervous systems. They too are benefited by the presence of someone radiating that Supreme Frequency, as if screaming it through the whole universe, the whole bottomless, fathomless, apex-less universe.

*Overcoming Mass Psychosis, June 25, 2005, DVD #12*

## When an Avatar Descends into a Human Birth

The word Avatar means descent.

When an Avatar descends into a human birth, there's a great explosion of Descending Energy.

That is, the Divine Consciousness finds a body-mind that will carry its force down into the human realm.

So, when that body descends and hits the earth, everyone on the earth goes up toward the Paramatman, toward the Supreme Consciousness.

And, while that Being is alive, they bring many beings up into the Light, even though they come from a Descending Energy, a Descending Force.

*The Field of Feeling, July 2, 2002, DVD #7*

# Even if You Feel Like You've Failed, This Is a Good Place to Come

There's no first and last. No one gets to earn this. No one can prove himself or herself more worthy. It's just an organic flowering from within. So, even if you've done practices in your life and you feel like you've failed, this is a good place to come. Or perhaps you've not failed, but you did not achieve what you had hoped for. Either your hopes were inaccurate or maybe you just needed a little more experience in Consciousness to give you the knowledge that you need about yourself.

Just take it easy. Don't let your depressed self get to you. Don't let your futile, terminally terrible disposition convince you of something prematurely, because you'll go through all kinds of mood swings on this path that make menopause look like a party. There are worse things than that.

There are tsunamis of transformation in the spiritual condition when you're losing your identity. You're losing your mind. You're losing your sanity as it's being reestablished back into its origin.

Often we need help from someone who has taken those steps and has survived and is still fairly sane at the end. They may not be totally sane, but you can still see they're functional. It gives you great hope, great courage. "If it can happen to that moron, it can happen to me." You get the sense that the teacher is not really that different from you.

Look what's happening in Consciousness now! It's beautiful!

*Talks and Dialog on the Internet, Volume 5, July 24, 2009*

# The Siddha Has This Very Deep Devotion to Have the Whole Transformation in Consciousness Take Place

I know of no Great Being who hasn't suffered their whole life to attain what they attained. They had to put everything on the line for that. And even within that there are all kinds of fears, and cowardice, and hesitation—even in the Great Beings. Even they fear what they are about to do or what they are trying to execute in their own consciousness. It's not that they are supermen. They just have this very deep devotion to have this whole transformation in consciousness take place and that's what keeps them rooted.

If you think there's an individual in back of the performance of siddhi, you've erred in your understanding. There is no individuality behind siddhi. Siddhi just means perfection. It's a display of perfection.

A Siddha is called a perfected being because his or her consciousness has evolved totally, not because he can do this, that, and this. "This, that, and this" might arise in the presence of a Siddha, an accomplished being, but he or she could care less. Within my teaching, there are teaching siddhis, such as what happened to you when you were listening to the interview, getting wired right into my entire teaching through some "dead" voice waves.

That's the display of an exemplary mastery, not by me, but within the Field in which I operate, which is enlivening and permeating my life-essence. I don't get high on saying that, in the sense of feeling important and special, not at all. It has nothing to do with self-importance. It has to do with the truth, and if these things arise in the context of the truth, then we have to account for them.

*Discussing Advaita, October 10, 2009, DVD #26*

## Some People Really Need a Devotional Connection with a Living Teacher

Realization is mostly dependent on the student. It's the student's devotion, desire and hunger that get met by the teacher. The teacher is always already giving everything at any moment. The question is, when you come into the room, are you completely focused on this? Are you completely aligned with either your own inner being or the mind of the teacher or both? Some people might really need a devotional connection with a living teacher. It's not enough just to go into the impersonal. It's not enough for some people. Perhaps some yogis, maybe they go into a cave, like Ramana Maharshi. He went to the cave, he sat down and, essentially he didn't get up for a long time. He wasn't running to teachers. He was happy with the impersonal, right? So, maybe one of us is a Ramana Maharshi and that's what we need to do. Others have Gurus. They have teachers and there is a great devotional connection—indispensable.

You have to really tune into what you need. You can't be thinking about what you "should" do, what the "proper" posture is. You've got to find your spiritual posture as you move into your realization. As you start to become enlightened, you start to know more, you start to know better.

For me, there's nothing higher than a human teacher,

a humanly realized teacher. To me, the Guru is better than God: Him—or Her—or Itself. The Guru is a million times better than any impersonal God. That's my humble opinion, but other people will feel differently.

*The Mind Is Complicit in Realization, May 29, 2011, DVD 3 37*


# This Transmission Becomes Your Own Self-Activating Bliss-Consciousness

*Participant:* I'm experiencing a deep, strong, heavy trance-like state, floating more and more.

*David:* So, when you use words like "trance-like" and "floating," you're really honing in on the qualities of the Absolute. You said "spacey" or "floating." That's the mind's reading of its own experience as it's honing in toward that Silence. The mind is affected. Thought is affected. The feeling in Being is affected, all toward expansion or non-differentiation. It's all moving toward the diffusion of particularized attention and the dawning of undifferentiated awareness. So, just know that and that this is part of what is supposed to happen.

*Participant:* Thank you. There is a very soft and embracing Transmission tonight, blue light everywhere.

*David:* All these different kinds of experiences—visual, color-based experience, energy, currents, rising/descending Shakti, deep unfolding silence, thoughtlessness, ascension in attention—all of these are magnificent symptoms of that Ocean, which is liberated, that Ocean which is now casting its vapor into your awareness.

Then, *the transport* happens as a result of real insight into Consciousness—the profusion, the affluence, of awareness itself, inundating.

*Participant:* Can the Transmission continue throughout the week?

*David:* Yes! It can continue forever. It may start off on the basis of minutes, hours, days, weeks and then your real vision should be focused on forever—so that this Transmission becomes your own Self-Activating Bliss-Consciousness. That's what mind's real root is. In me it's Self-Activating Bliss-Consciousness. It's my "Me." My "Me" is Consciousness—Awakened, Full, and Absolute. So, when you're coming into this with me, that's the Field that you are also coming into, within you. We can't separate ourselves at that point.

*Participant:* There's a loss of contraction and loss of definition of a 'me,' a unitary perception of all kaleidoscopic color, Bliss, all effortless, with complete understanding.

*David:* It's that simple and that easy.

You can see me as a frequency generator, generating many, many frequencies simultaneously. And each of you, then, has an opportunity, a thread, of that Transmission-Power thrown to you. It's offered to you. And once you find it you begin to have a direct relationship with me in a Universal Field. Each thread is like an individual yoga. It's an individual path and an infinite number of such threads can be cast, not just now, not just here; and depending on the depth of your connection with my teaching, an infinite number of possibilities arise as to what can happen.

If you have the time to meditate a little bit after this gathering (and it won't interfere with your sleep or your life in any way, your schedule), go ahead and sit. And if that Bliss is aggregated around you, give it some time to permeate in something of a formal meditation. Let it enlarge you, your consciousness, and you'll see that it's really about you. It's not just about me as transmitter. It's also about you as absorber. They have equal importance and really the teaching is about you taking on the full stature of the source of my Transmission, you taking it on and letting it become a permanent aspect of your own awareness.

Now, that's not going to happen overnight. But it will happen slowly if you're patient and you're attentive. If you're sincere and you have deep clarity, you'll begin to come into some kind of stabilization of our relationship—a stabilization, then, which will be about your Consciousness.

*Talks and Dialog on the Internet, Volume 3, December 16, 2008*

# The Teacher Is Simply Magnifying What Is Already Occurring in Your Life

What is the purpose of a teacher? What is the purpose of an awakened teacher? The teacher is simply magnifying what is already occurring in your life. The teacher does not add any outer element into your existence that isn't already latently present. He or she cannot create something within you.

Again, that innocence does not allow for the functioning of duality. What the teacher does is like what the sun does to plants. It comes out and in the presence of that warmth and light the plant goes into foliage. It goes into growth, spontaneous growth that is not pre-programmed by the sun. The sun just shines. The plant absorbs this cosmic energy and it begins to move in its own pre-destined direction.

There's such a great influx of Energy and Consciousness when we sit together. It's going to activate something in you, spontaneously, just the way the sun will activate a plant or a flower or a living thing. All living things need the sun. So, we are coming into the Sun of the Self, the Sun of Pure Consciousness, the Sun of Life, the Sun of Being.

All of those words are extraneous. We're not developing a philosophy here. Tomorrow, I could give a talk and contradict everything I said today. It doesn't matter what I say. But, if you follow it with innocence it will have a direction and it will have meaning and it will carry the Shakti, the force of Consciousness, the force of evolution.

What a teacher does is activate you from within yourself in a state of non-dual innocence. This may sound shocking, but what climaxes in such an Awakened Atmosphere is the realization that all that can and will happen to you, all that has happened to you, the essence of it, will occur today, in this Activated Moment.

Any way you can be brought into this awakening will be activated here. We're going way out now all of a sudden, away from the field of logic. The Awakened Consciousness will open your heart in an innocent way and just simply have it appreciate that opening, that it's there, and as a result of that, anything can happen. You can move into this condition forever or you can taste it and go out and get more experiences in the world. There's no good and no bad, no winning and no losing. Whatever happens is for your own good. It's spontaneously generated. It's a fact that may be known today. It may be known next week. It may be known in some future birth. It may be known next month. It doesn't matter.

It's difficult for human beings to understand that the very reason for their birth is to awaken to what they already are. It's very insulting to the logical mind that devises plans of action, plans of what to become—that everything you are right now is actually sufficient to your existence. You don't need to attain anything. You don't need to go anywhere. Yet we find ourselves going places. We find ourselves attaining things. That's just life.

You can never box this thing in with the mind. You can never hold on to this ultimate state of Being and Consciousness. It's not a thing. By the time it's written down, it's dead.

So, all the saviors and all the messiahs are dead. If you want a savior, you've got to become that yourself. You've got to become the messiah. Hmm—sounds too formidable? Does that scare you? It scares a lot of people. This is dangerous talk.

I wonder if you feel this Shakti, this Fire that's moving. It has no meaning other than what it is in itself. It has no destination. It's not there to enlighten you into some book-based enlightenment that you read about. A lot of people are having real enlightenment experiences. Some people are totally enlightened. But they've read too many books and then their book knowledge gets in the way. They can't look honestly and simply at their experience. They don't listen simply to what's being offered in their subjectivity, and they lose it, they lose that sublimity. They lose that profound quality of innocent Bliss.

I'm on fire with this. It's from here to here (pointing heart to heart). It's not from here to here (pointing head to head). You know that. It's really in the guts that I'm talking, not out of my head. You're with me—good. Do you feel this Energy? Good.

Whatever happens in here is just regulated spontaneously. It's kind of like a thermostat on the air conditioner. When it gets to a certain level and the group is happy that way, it will kind of shut off for a while. And then, if there's a big yearning in the group to go higher, it will get generated into the "on" position again and more Transmission will come. But, for the most part, it's intuitive and self-regulating. It's not about doing anything on my part.

*The Sun of Being, May 29, 2004, DVD #8*

[Green Tara]

No devious approach to getting enlightened will ever produce it. But the Openness, the Silence of Love, does produce the fruition of awakening. It produces it from within itself so that you are simultaneously freed from your "me," freed from the demanding consciousness that makes you suffer, that is suffering.

part [6]

# Realization

## Yellow Buddha

In the wilderness
    of an extreme interiority

I devoured the conditions of the world like a lion
    and all humanness seemed to fly from me

    like mosquitos from a galloping horse
whose sweat was sweet with unbridled movement

            (His tears were round and few
                aching from the belly
                    of a yellow Buddha)

    Now the world cries for the softness of my palm,
                in the center of which sits a stone,
            like the egg of something yet to be born

[1977]

# The Beauty of Innocence

The Awakened Heart has this quality of innocence already established in it. It has natural curiosity. It accepts no answer as final, no experience as ultimate. It will not accept some absolute answer.

So the very nature of the innocent, curious mind is kept fully intact in the Awakened Condition. It's something to be felt right in the heart.

So, each time we come here, we start afresh in that innocence, that love. It's such a beautiful thing to know this intuitively, without the mind, that inherently there is this already present Love, which has activated Energy in it: Awakened Consciousness.

Its foundation is in the non-dual plane of Pure Consciousness.

It's an amazing thing that when we listen from this plane of innocence, in this meditation in the Awakened Heart, in this gathering that we hold once a week here, it's as if I'm speaking to each individual.

There is a peculiar kind of relationship that's forged in this innocent awareness that gives one the feeling that it's just for you. It's just for your Self. That feeling comes about because of a lack of duality, the lack of feeling of otherness, of others, of objects, of things. It comes about because there is this inherently felt oneness.

Right in this moment, you can feel the self-activating nature of the Shakti, which is meditation, which is Vedanta.

Just as the waves of the ocean are not different from the vastness of its depth, so too the moving Shakti is not different from the Ultimate Consciousness, which is fully non-dual—without difference, without subject, without object.

Right now, in this moment, you can feel this fire activated and moving spontaneously without any human involvement.

*The Beauty of Innocence, April 22, 2003, DVD # W-2*

# In Awakening, Consciousness Possesses the Body-Mind

There's no difference between awakening and suffering. The Infinite Consciousness continues to revel in desire long after Self-Awakening, after Nirvikalpa Samadhi, after full Transcendental Realization.

The difference is that Consciousness now has gripped this body-mind that is full of the Love-Light and has its way with it. It possesses that body-mind.

Consciousness becomes the resident along with all the other relative aspects of the personality: the ego, the mind, the intellect, the senses, and the emotions. So, all of those relative dimensions have adjusted themselves, surrendered themselves to the presence of this Awakened Consciousness.

Every cell of the body-mind is sipping this Nectar of

Enlightened-Feeling, Awakened-Feeling, Heart-Feeling.

*The Ocean of Liberated Bliss, April 16, 2002, DVD #59*

# Samadhi, Transcendental Awareness, Is Here!

Right in this moment, the Life-Shakti, the currents of energy and delight, are activated. Samadhi, Transcendental Awareness, is here!

At some point, if you're graced by good fortune, the experience of That and the conviction of That, even the mere mental conviction of it, become one.

Until that magic moment appears, the body-mind must simply unravel its story, its bliss-tragedy story. It must unravel and reveal its inherent story to itself, until all meaning is transcended, until all content is transcended.

At some point, even God is transcended.

So that there's no history. There's no personal history and there's no intellectual history that you have memorized from any kind of textbook, spoken or written.

Your own life becomes the living reality that you study now, that you speak about, that you interact within, that you offer as a gift.

*The Ocean of Liberated Bliss, April 16, 2002, DVD #59*

# The Entire Human Journey Culminates in Nothingness

Isn't it odd that the entire human journey culminates in returning to a state of Nothingness, a state of Silence, without any action in it?

You would think that all this activity amounts to something, means something, goes somewhere and accomplishes something. But, in fact, it's just the expression of Nothing. It is Nothing.

So, action is purposeless effulgence. That's the real meaning of action. It's purposeless joy in the field of perception, thought, feeling, thinking, relationship, and touch, when all of those elements come together in a kind of wholeness of the Awakened Self.

Then, what is engaged is Divine Relationship. Divine Relationship is not some special kind or type of relationship. It's the fullness of Feeling that happens in the state of Nothingness, when the mind and the body come into contact with the external world.

*The Field of Feeling, July 2, 2002, DVD #7*

# There Is Nothing Personal in Enlightenment

There is nothing personal in enlightenment.

Enlightenment, we could say, is a vast Emptiness, an impersonal backdrop and it certainly does not destroy the functioning of the personality or ego-structure, or the feelings, or bodily functioning. But it is prior to all of that.

The body-mind might get an intimation that enlightenment has in fact occurred, which is that the subtlest level of the mind has somehow become enlightened about the nature of the presence/non-presence of this Field, that it somehow agrees it exists—not agrees in the sense of believes, or has faith in the fact it exists, but is utterly reconciled and aligned toward that Field. I don't say "in" that Field because nothing enters into it.

It's important to note that the structure of the personality remains intact. This bears repeating. Everything continues as it was. Nothing changes in the relative. Many of the likes and dislikes that were present before awakening are still present afterwards, unless there was some recognition of some kind of negativity in one's habit patterns, in which case there might be a quick adjustment, a quick and spontaneous adjustment in behavior.

Phenomena like calmness, peace, even the feeling of non-duality, are all outside of the Enlightened Field. The personality, the ego-structure, might *think* it knows only because it feels the wave-like undulations, the pulsations of Quietness, Energy and Love that happen near that Emptiness.

But, that Emptiness exists nowhere near the human personality. It's good to understand this completely, beacuse it teaches you not to attach to any form of experience that arises.

This might be perceived as a letdown. You might feel deflated as a result of knowing this kind of thing because— if it's not for the "me" and if it doesn't come to bear on relative existence—then what is this and what's the point of it? There's a passionate movement toward the truth in someone who desires to have it revealed to him. That movement is created by life itself. There is no selfish motive in it.

So, the notion that enlightenment can work for you, or you can extract something out of it, is foreign to the very process of true awakening. They just don't exist in that spectrum. Of course, it might be inevitable that the ego-mind thinks and can't help but think that there's something there for it. Ironically, it may be a kind of deluded selfishness that occurs alongside a genuine and spontaneous awakening process, one that is motivated by nature.

The separate "me" will continue to interpret everything in that strange fashion only because that's the field in which it has comprehension—in the field of the "me" versus the object, in duality. So it sees everything as a reflection of what it wants or doesn't want. But real enlightenment is something that we don't ever really know, except through the feeling of fulfillment that comes from its own realization.

It's a fulfillment that can't be described or experienced in any other way. You can't miss it for something else. Even the human personality has an intuition about this. It senses "the Other." It senses where the personality begins and ends. It knows where birth and death exist, and therefore, by default, knows what That is. But it never knows where That is positively. It never positively affirms That in personal consciousness. It's only by virtue of what it is not that you know that it is there in what has been realized. It's what the "me" can't know about it that enlightens the "me" as to its presence.

It's good to hear this kind of information because it helps the ego-mind to have a "hands-off" approach when it comes to realizing the impersonal. Hands off! Just to hear that knowledge will instruct the relative personality. In that way, you're guided subtly to a correct approach, a correct posture in relationship to your own spontaneously occurring sadhana.

*Enlightenment Is Not for the "Me," July, 3, 2009, DVD #26*

# The Magnification of Light—
# Not Merely the Grinding Away of the
# Sense of "Me"—Will Create a Whole New
# Understanding and Way to Realize God

The customary understanding of the path of awakening is that it's difficult, strenuous. It's the erosion of the small self until it becomes so miniscule, so thin and translucent that the Ultimate Reality can shine through. That's one understanding of it. You could also reverse the understanding of that and say that it's the magnification of Light to the point that no density can opaque it out, no density can shut out the magnificence of the Light.

So, if the magnification of Light then is the reason for enlightenment, and not merely the grinding away of the sense of "me," then a whole new understanding, one based more upon pleasure, can dawn—one that transcends the idea that renunciation, active, willful renunciation—is the way to realize God.

To reverse traditional understandings is a necessary act for the communication of real enlightenment—to reinvent language, reinvent how the understanding works, reinvent the very atmosphere in which apprehension of the Divine takes place. Those are the characteristics of an awakened atmosphere, what is commonly referred to as "satsang." "Satsang" points to the reality, the clarity, that awakening may be apprehended in a group, directly, through atmospheric transformation, or transfiguration, or illuminessence. That is what I was pointing to previously: the magnification of Light, the Light of Consciousness, or the Self.

There's no particular posture or mood the listener needs to adopt in order to receive the influx of Light here. Any internal posture is welcomed and permitted based on the nature of this teaching.

The transmission of Consciousness is not transmitted from one self to another. However, it becomes permissible for someone who is sufficiently intoxicated with the Divine to refer to himself in the first person as Consciousness.

So, for me to say that I, as Consciousness, meditate you, can be understood correctly to mean that Consciousness is arising in a Single Field, but is expressed dualistically.

In this particular context, our feelings come together in this "satsang" atmosphere, this group consciousness, held together by a tiny strand of Light, so to speak, a Light which is pinpoint or threadlike in size, but which contains the whole Ocean of Universal Consciousness. And as that thread weaves itself, symbolically speaking, through the attendees, through the recipients or the Heart-Friends, the Divine-Friends, then there is a singular, overwhelming stimulation of the entire energy in each consciousness, in each being, in every being simultaneously.

If you move together, both as a group and with me in your understanding, we will be like soldiers walking through a mine field, or like a flock of birds flying together. The soldiers can, by simply paying attention to the one who knows which areas to stay away from, elude every mine, and no casualties occur. Or, like the lead bird that moves one or two degrees to the right and everything goes instantaneously with it. There's no thought in such movement, there's no duality in such movement, even though it appears to be a totally dualistic situation.

So, if you could learn to listen like that, riding the subtle nuances of meaning and feeling within yourself, ensconced in this Divine Energy; knowing, feeling, and experiencing the power of meditation and the communication of awakening, then something really grand is destined to happen. Something is meant to happen here, something that is naturally the outcome of being here, not something that's attained by you through some subtle effort on your own part to see or understand a certain way, but something that actually comes to fruition organically.

No devious approach to getting enlightened will ever produce it. But the Openness, the Silence of Love, does produce the fruition of awakening. It produces it from within itself so that you are simultaneously freed from your "me," freed from the demanding consciousness that makes you suffer, that is suffering.

It's not necessary to mechanically deconstruct and eradicate that tendency forever. It's only necessary to see through it for prolonged durations of time or to exist in an atmosphere where That has already seen through and is constantly radiated. So, yes, you can "achieve" realization and you can also be realized by the atmosphere itself, in which all of your karmas become insignificant barriers, like the soldiers who walk through that minefield and do not step on any mines.

They move with intelligence. They move with care. They move with heightened awareness that death is very close and that alertness keeps them meticulously in the field of pure attention, and that attention is what is actually guiding the leader. It's not his knowledge of mine fields. Yes, he has to have some knowledge of how mine fields are structured, what the nature of the mines are, how they blow up, like the teacher has some understanding about the nature of desire, the nature of identification, how suffering occurs, how bondage is birthed and maintained in an individual.

I want to replicate what I've realized in every person who sits with me, regardless of what your philosophy or spiritual beliefs are. I have no interest in manufacturing a particular kind of understanding in the people that sit with me, precisely the opposite. I would first invite you to lovingly abandon, as you would in falling in love, all previous understandings that you've held so dear, so what's actually navigating your mind is that Awakened Consciousness.

*Understand and Experience Reality, December 17, 2005, DVD #17*

# Liberation Is a Condition-Less Condition

What is termed liberation is a spiritual condition that is not a condition. Please, listen carefully. I'm not giving you clichés. I'm offering you a fresh understanding, based on intuition, the intuition of what that condition, that condition-less condition, is. You could say that it is something that is not graspable by the mind.

Think of the mind as always grasping with its understanding. Think of mind as a form of grasping, just as when you grasp an object. The mind is unable to release itself from its own impulse to grasp.

That's a fact. So release must come from liberation itself, not revealed to the mind as a state in which a certain message or experience is contained, but as a simple interaction of the mind with its Source. We must be very careful not to posit that Source as an object. To snap that habit, one needs only clear awareness itself, upon which all that grasping is occurring, to breathe into the mind, which would not be the interaction of one state with another.

Enlightenment is not the replacement of a suffering state by a liberated state. It's not the superimposition of one state of being upon another. All that is rightly called duality. So, if you're wondering why certain religions have insisted that grasping come to an end, it's because the mind can't grasp it. But what these religions have failed to conceive is that you can't turn non-grasping into a path toward the ungraspable.

So, instead of simply understanding that it's beyond grasping, aspirants are told to learn how to stop grasping, when all you need to do is really hear and understand and accept completely, with your whole intelligence, that it can't be grasped, that it simply lies beyond the field of taking or grasping.

So then, other practices are introduced such as quelling desire, bringing thought to an end, all the practices that then tend to actually reinforce the state of separation.

So, the best and most immediate way to understand what liberation is—is to just liberate.

*Understanding Liberation, October 13, 2009, DVD*

# To Get That Fulfilled Feeling, You've Got to Go to the Limit, You've Got to Become Everything

Consciousness is always with you. When it shows its face and says, "I'm always here," don't look the other way and say, "No, I'm going to wait for David." You'd better take it. At some point, you're going to self-combust. It's going to happen just by witnessing this again and again. This whole thing is going to implant itself in you. So that one day you're going to wake up and realize the Divine is worshiping itself in you, as you. It's cool. There's no higher God than you. There's no higher Being, no higher Self. There's no other universe. There's no heaven. There's you, as Self-Activating Bliss-Consciousness.

All the different steps of worship that you see acted out externally in puja worship in India, for example, all of that is internalized as an awakening experience. So, the Supreme God of the universe uses your body-mind as an altar, your emotions, your intellect—all of what you are—to realize what He or She or It is. It's good stuff.

So, you never find some paradisal land of nothingness where you're safe and protected and never suffer again. Nirvana is when you become basically sane enough to go insane again. Nirvana is just exiting the dream of the changing, coming into the static awareness of transcendental, absolute Being, knowing that that changing realm was hideously false. But, you don't remain there. You can't hold onto that. It's just a feature of Being. It's just another polarity.

So, you continue until all of you becomes the Living Divine, all of you becomes God. Then, you have no need for God. You can drop all that language. You can fulfill it and you drop it. You won't need anything beyond that point. You'll just be That. You'll walk in it. You'll sleep in it. And then the antithesis will be there. You're not it and you're just a miserable individual who is born and is going to die. You have that, too. You have all of it. It's really bad!

*Participant:* What's the alternative?

*David:* There is no alternative. The alternative is to just live in some small part of your psyche. In the awakening process people just go deliciously mad. They hear and they see everything and that's neither good nor bad. It's not ugly. It's not beautiful. But there's something about it that tastes of everything and that's the taste that, apparently, all human beings are really hungry for. Until then, ice cream is there and it still tastes good. But it's not giving you what you want. Sex is still there. It tastes good. But even that's not giving you what you want. It gives you something, but that something is not fulfilling you. To get that fulfilled feeling, you've got to go to the limit. You've got to become everything. You just have to do it, just the way a bird learns to fly. You learn to do it by listening to me or someone like me. You get somebody who's transmitting, who's radiating 24/7, in Vast Cosmic Fields, in all directions, and that's how you get it. You'll get it by paying attention to your life in the context of a relationship like that.

It could take a long time, even with that relationship, have no doubt. You just don't know. It could take six weeks, six minutes, six years, six lifetimes. You just don't know, which means you've got to get over this idea that you're going somewhere, you're getting something out of this, that this is a finished end product.

It's every second that counts. It's who you are, authentically, in every second. That's all that counts and you can't turn that into a practice. You can't turn authenticity into a practice. That's just the ultimate form of hypocrisy. Just listen to what I'm saying. I'm not going to deliver you, but that Energy might. Just listen and feel. Let your heart open. Let your head fall. Be-head yourself. You'll feel good. You'll feel relieved of yourself.

When you start to feel that unique Presence and Fulfillment, that everything has been revealed, even a flash of it, that it doesn't need to stay 24/7—then you're beginning to breathe in the Ultimate.

*Participant:* I'm beginning to see that that includes feeling like shit, too.

*David:* Of course it does! You can feel like "shit" and it's okay.

But you've got to map this out so that you are getting your realization, as it's coming to you, at every step. So, when it is, "I am completely free from all suffering," you've got to get that. And you've got to get it as, "that's going to be absolutely and irrevocably true."

*Participant:* And could you still be suffering at the same time?

*David:* No, there is no 'and' to that. In other words, it's an unqualified realization at every step. You've got to believe in your own process. You can't ask me outside of your own movement towards self-confidence. I can only marry you in the place where you believe you're God, not in the place where you don't believe you're God.

*Reality is Nowhere, January 5, 2010, DVD #27*

# Working Tantrically in Consciousness with Rage, Desire, Fear, Anger, and Sadness

*Participant:* I'm really scared to feel that anger in myself because it's like physical danger.

*David:* Yes, it's dangerous.

*Participant:* You don't know what's going to happen if you feel that anger.

*David:* It's not about extroverting anger or rage. It's about letting it, with its tremendous energy and force, simply make you real in your apprehension. It's all about working tantrically in Consciousness with these rages—with desire, with fear, anger, sadness. If you want to work tantrically with these things, it means that they have to occur in the Open Space of Being.

I'm talking here about tantric understanding. I'm interested in talking to you in a very direct way, in a way that I would only with my closest friends. I'm not pretending to be beyond any kind of feeling myself, in some spacious place where I'm beyond anger or I'm beyond sex. I'm not "beyond" anything. And I'm not just saying this to make myself look "good," so you doubly love me. I really am nothing, really. I'm just despicable, actually. I'm just what you see. Do you understand?

And I love this stuff, too. I love this [stroking a Quan Yin statue]. There's no contradiction in my mind. I can be all of this. I can be the devotee. I can be the meditator. All of this is in my Being. I'm the Supreme Absolute in human form, if you want to use that language, not because I decided it one day. I didn't get up out of bed and say, "Oh, what a great idea, I'll try that." It's because it was in my face. It was apparent. Everything was That. Everything was Consciousness. There was no non-Consciousness. There was no non-God. It was forced on me. It's not an ideal state. You wouldn't want it. You wouldn't want realization. You think you do when you read the books, "Oh yeah, I'd like to have my third eye opened."

In our naiveté, we run after fantasies and it's okay. That's part of the bhakti path, to run after fantasies. I did that. I still do it. I can still go into bhakti reverie if I want and yet I have this other side. Then I'm Kali—get rid of all the bhakti, no bhakti!

It's fun. Try it. Life can become interesting. You have all these different textures to your totality. I'm suggesting you can do this. I don't know if you can, but I'm going to make it sound like you can. I have to believe that what I am, you are also. I can't reserve this for me. It's not mine. It would be a lie to imply that. It would be deceptive and insane.

So, you are who you are. I really like that. I just like you for being who you are, not your ego self. I mean, that's just a bunch of conditioned shit and there's nothing there.

My ego's pretty permeated actually. It's very strange. The ego's pretty translucent. So when I get angry, it's like a magical arm comes out and punches in the Absolute.

163

Imagine some little spider in my head with all these legs and one is anger, one is rage, one is lust. Instead of going out into the senses and having to have the object, I simply puncture Being with it. The intensity of my expression is not a personal thing and there's no anger actually—believe it or not. I'm actually free of anger.

*Participant:* It's a ferocity.

*David:* Yes, it's a fierceness. It's like a dog growling. But it's the same dog that you were kissing and letting lick your face just a minute ago. Is the growl real or not? It's just a different structure in that dog's apprehension and consciousness. It's a face of its being. But you don't stereotype it as always growling simply because it growled once.

*Participant:* So, now when you go into a political tirade, I'm not even listening to the politics.

*David:* Just get the Energy, exactly. That's all I'm doing. I'm always teaching, honestly. It's all about me trying to offer you something new and fresh every moment, especially if you have this idea that anger is not in enlightenment. Then, I've got to show you that. That would be the best teaching of all for you.

I'm not joking now. How much energy you do have to put into your perseverance? How much natural hunger do you have for this? To what extreme are you willing to go? You don't have to factually go there. But, you know, are you available and ready to go anywhere, to do anything, to taste this? Are you in that form of readiness? Are you possessed by your Life-Current to that extent?

It's an interesting question, not just a question, but a terrible, confrontational issue. It's not that you have to come out feeling like a hypocrite (if you don't have the energy). If you don't have the energy, then you just are honest with yourself. Then you live with that for a while and something beautiful happens because you care for it as what you are. You can't pretend you're something different.

*Reality is Nowhere, January 5, 2010, DVD #27*

# The Dissolving Power of the Awakened Heart

In the logic of time and space, that is, the logic of the body, the human nervous system and the finite mind, with its logic and reason, there are many so-called obstacles to becoming this Infinite Consciousness, this unlimited freedom, this full identity with the Absolute Consciousness.

Yet, the most natural thing is actually to become one's Self. It's the easiest thing, the most lovable thing of all.

In the presence of an Awakened Being, who has come into the full feeling of the Heart, the Heart-Consciousness, these so-called obstacles, whether they are real or imagined, can be transcended rapidly.

That means there is a dissolving power that emanates out of the Awakened Heart—the power of dissolution itself. This dissolution impacts, penetrates, into the body-mind of the recipient, the Heart-Friend, and melts the density that seems to prevent Heart-Awakening from occurring.

*The Ocean of Liberated Bliss, April 16, 2002, DVD #59*

# The Spiritual Master's Attention Replaces Your Attention

Consciousness is already liberated. It's attention that requires liberation, and that means just displacing the center of attention. Ordinarily the center of attention is lodged in a feeling of separate-consciousness, separative awareness. It lodges there, and then all it sees is difference. It sees only differences. So, once you liberate attention from that nasty contraction, it begins to realize Consciousness very quickly.

One of the symptoms of the liberation of attention is Bliss. You begin to feel a wave of Bliss come over you. The Bliss is the sense of relief that happens in the body-mind as it is extricated from duality. It's a beautiful feeling, like diving into a cool lake when you're very, very hot.

It has a nectar-like feeling to it and that Bliss is also Freedom—the freedom from otherness, from being bound to the sense that there are others, that there's another place, another state, another world. So, when this feeling dissolves, this congested feeling of attention being bound with otherness, there's a wonderful feeling about it, something happens to the Heart.

The nature of that transformation, from bound attention to Liberated Consciousness, is in the dissolution of a solid sense of separation that exists in the jiva, in the inner self, in the "I." So, the radiant and diffusive nature of Consciousness, as it's flowing through attention, dissolves the separation of attention from the contents of consciousness and produces just Consciousness.

Attention is concentrated Consciousness. It's in the nature of attention to move. Attention can actually dissolve duality. It relaxes and releases us back into the Bliss of Being. See it happening now! It's actually happening. What I'm describing, it's happening now.

We can all partake of the communion of our own consciousnesses in the one Single-Consciousness in which we all are already established. How this happens is a great mystery, how the power within realization itself can communicate itself in all directions, even over vast distances.

You can become liberated in two basic ways. One way is by turning within, away from all outer aspects or objects, and dissolving into the root of your attention, in which no teacher or spiritual transmission is necessary. But I must also say that it is quite rare for anyone to just pick up this kind of process on their own, to pick up this kind of talent for dissolving their own identity.

The second way is through becoming inundated with Spiritual Transmission from someone who is radiating that entirety of Consciousness. It's as if the Transmission of the teacher functions as Grace to bestow the liberation that you are seeking. The Spiritual Master's attention replaces your attention and in that way the teacher can be the dispenser of Grace and Freedom and Liberation. The key is to connect with the teacher.

Spiritual Transmission, the reception of it and also the giving of it, is all spontaneous. It's more important that you discover that it is possible, not just take my word for it, as an authority, but actually begin to come into this relationship that's already ongoing.

Come into the feeling of Consciousness right now, the feeling of it. Don't look for it with your mind or your eyes or even your attention. Just rest in that place where you feel, where Feeling is. That's the place where we will meet.

It's elegant. It's simple. It's without complication. No effort is required. No doing is required. It's just the capacity of your own Consciousness to arise through the process of your listening. So, just be patient and watch what's happening. It's happening now. Attention is on fire, burning.

So don't get too caught up trying to understand this. This is not an intellectual matter. It's something to just discover right now. Just find the place where we're on the same continuum. You can do that.

Remember, I said reside in Feeling, reside in the place where Feeling is. You don't have to look for that place. Nor should you try to dissociate from what is going on inside of you. Just leave everything alone. Leave yourself alone and watch a new quality in awareness come to be.

*Talks and Dialog on the Internet, Volume 1, April 30, 2008,*
*DVD #I-1*

# The Key Is to Give Yourself over Completely to Your Spiritual Experience

The key is to just give yourself over completely to your spiritual experience, merge into what you know. Merge into what you experience so that you are not looking at it from the outside. You perfect a kind of homogenization of your experience and your understanding by naturally giving yourself into it. That's called surrender. It's releasing yourself into Consciousness. Do it now. Don't wait for tomorrow. Do it with me now. This is the best place to do this kind of thing.

The less you are, the more we can be together in Consciousness, until there's only One. You could call that One the Self, your Self, your Being, or you could call it God, or the Guru, or the Absolute, depending on your aesthetic preference, what feels right in your case. Some people who adore the impersonal only want to think of it in terms of Consciousness, the Absolute, the "One without a second." Those who are devotionally inclined adore it as the Creator or Creatrix. And those who are both devotionally and exceptionally emotionally inclined adore it as the Guru, as the Master in physical form. One understanding is just as valid as the other. It's only what resonates in your total process of feeling that allows you to choose the correct understanding and that will be done naturally.

Our connection should be so powerful, even after just one or two meetings, that you should feel like something significant has happened that can never be undone. There's a sense of great, great connection, profound, to the point where it dissolves your fears. Do what you need to do on your end and the Grace is always coming toward you in all directions.

*Talks and Dialog on the Internet, Volume 1, April 30, 2008,*
*DVD #I-1*

# If Desire Is Knotted, with the Loving, Unconditional Apprehension of Your True Self, Which Is No-Self, Begin to Undo the Knot

When you're dealing with the paradoxical, you're dealing in a field of mystery. You're dealing in a field of joyful unknowingness and the most you can do is align your thinking and speaking, emoting and loving, and your whole visceral life energy into that unknowableness. It's a process of spontaneous alignment in consciousness with That which is totally infinite and manifesting as your finiteness. It is both at the same time. It is the infinite expanse of unknowingness and it is the particularized movement of your own individuality.

When you sense restriction coming in, constriction, limitation and that unique suffering that is due to the suppression of feeling, then you need to know how to backtrack, move inside, and simply go prior to that constrictive energy, that constrictive movement. It can be done, but it's intuitive. It's grasped moment by moment.

You find where desire is knotted, and then you go there and with the loving, unconditional apprehension of your true Self, which is no-self, you begin to undo the knot, the constriction. You let it come undone. Sometimes it can be accompanied by catharsis, by an emotional release. It can be undone without much effort at all.

So, if you are becoming hyper-energized and there is too much spiritual energy, then you need to go beyond that too. You need to go beyond the Shakti into the total silence of the Self. If there is not enough peace and equanimity, go into meditation, access that place in your consciousness that is quiet and free and peaceful, easy, easy.

It's a great struggle sometimes to capture this livingness. You can't capture it.

It's like walking a dog. The dog ends up walking you most of the time, but it's like a battle between who's getting the best of whom at any given time. It's kind of an agreement, a subtle agreement process you make between you and the dog that…. I mean, how can you reason with a dog? You can't really make an agreement. You just walk it and hope that there are some joyful steps that are taken together, because the dog may pull in this direction or in that direction. You know how they are.

When working with this Infinite Consciousness, there's not much you can do, except just exude, on a non-verbal level, your connection with That. Then, if you can say a few coherent words to give an indication that this freedom in Consciousness is the case, that this has occurred in you in a way that takes into consideration the needs of the person that's listening, then a remarkable thing happens in your communication process. Then you are actually talking from the heart of both people at the same time and that produces instantaneous transformation. It's quite amazing.

Not enough can be said about this, about how to communicate lovingly, delicately, tactfully, in a state where desire is absolutely limitless. It's come into its limitless quality, and at the same time it's still functioning in its own movement, its own individualized movement in space and time.

Don't get all uptight and uncomfortable because you are in the process of desire, because desire always means duality and duality means conflict. Just don't let that bother you. Don't pay attention to that aspect. Just function through it. Function in it. It's okay. You accept it, just as you accept yourself. You just accept things as they are and you find that that acceptance breeds a tremendous freedom.

*The Innocence of Not Knowing, October 2, 2004, DVD #12*

# The Questioner Is Not Different than the Question

Remember, the questioner is not different than the question.

You're never really asking *about*. You're asking *as*.

Do you see the difference in those prepositions?

You're not asking to be informed about what you're asking.

You're asking to become what you are asking about.

So, it doesn't have to be a magnificent question about the nature of the cosmos, just a very simple communication of your urgency, whatever that is.

*The Field of Feeling, July 2, 2002, DVD #7*

# I Don't Want to Even be "Enlightened" When I Come in This Room

If you want absolute peace you'd have to sit in samadhi all the time, never talk and hardly eat. But, once you enter into the active phase of living, it's full of problems, real ones and imagined ones, and don't try to figure out which are which. Just solve them or move on.

So, you're not even in a position to predict what's going to happen to you from moment to moment. Even tonight, I didn't feel like coming here. I felt like watching TV. You know, it's turning out to be such an exquisite evening. It's really one of those rare evenings that I look forward to so much. But it was just given in the moment and when we all leave it's just going to evaporate again. Except I don't have this thing that clings, that says that must be the case next time. I get totally emptied out of everything, even of expectation. So, the next time I come, I'm all stupid again—all for you.

You see, I don't want to even be "enlightened" when I come in this room. That's too much baggage. I'm just as I am. I'm just who I am. And that includes the relative "me" and the absolute "me." So, remember that now. You're just who you are from moment to moment. You don't have to be the big Self. Don't lay that one on you. That's the last trip to go, the enlightenment trip.

*Talks and Dialog on the Internet, Volume 5, July 24, 2009, DVD #I-5*

# Awakening Is Better Spoken of as Blossoming-Power than the Mere, Dry Term, "Enlightenment"

All the religions are mythical, symbolic. They are parables or poems about this Reality. But this is not a poem. This is not a parable. This is the actual display of it. And the mechanics of its communication, from one human being to another, is osmosis. It's what lights one candle from another. The warmth of that burning can be transferred from one heart to another. Why? Because it's only natural to do so. It's a natural communication. It's like the fragrance of a flower. It's like the vision of a beautiful sunset. It's lovingly communicated, spontaneously, through the agencies within nature, through the mechanics of nature itself. And so, it's from one organic being to another. It's from one living consciousness to another.

I say "to another." I don't really mean that. But in order to talk coherently I have to act as though it goes from one place to another. In fact, if you sit here long enough something will be totally transformed in you, something that wasn't there to begin with. So, something did go from somewhere to somewhere else. Remember, it's both non-dual and dual.

Some people get into the trap of pointing merely to the non-dualistic nature of enlightenment, which is that nothing can be said about it. Nothing can summarize it verbally. All of that is accurate. It's absolutely true.

At the same time, the opposite is also true. Something can be said about it. Something should be said about it. And what can be said and what should be said are what arises naturally in a person's experience, as it has occurred. And if the experience is established in that Being, and the communication is eloquent and faithful to the experience, then something precious might happen to those who listen. Something precious will happen, if not today then tomorrow. If not tomorrow, then next year. You can't put a conventional time frame, or promise, or guarantee a certain time frame, for awakening to occur. It just occurs. It occurs when all of you is ready to receive it. That's all that can be said.

There are people who go on practicing for years and decades—and if you believe in lifetimes, lifetimes—and don't get it. It's not a fault of theirs. They're not defective. There's nothing wrong with them. But there is a particular kind of flowering that occurs only rarely in a human being, in its fullness and totality. And the perfume of that will be so overwhelming and intoxicating that others will be moved into that same blossoming. And so awakening is better spoken of as Blossoming-Power, Fragrance-Expansion, than the merely dry term, enlightenment.

Enlightenment is an awfully literalistic piece of language. It sounds like something you'd have done to your car or refrigerator. It has no love in it. But when we talk about the osmosis of mutual blossoming or aesthetic mutuality in Bliss, it has a whole a whole different fragrance. It has a whole beautiful movement to it, which is why religious teachings are quite sordid. They try to be literal expressions of something that is meant to be carried poetically. It should have beauty in it. We should have love to speak of this thing, which is beyond all things, which is not a thing.

Human beings can attain this reality only if the conditions are right and proper for them, which means that they are filled with an enormous amount of spiritual experience and a vast amount of worldly experience. Worldly experience means pleasure and pain. Spiritual experience means samadhi, Shakti, Silence, detachment, Bliss, Light, whichever realities appear to you. They won't appear in the same amount, in the same ratios, for all people. Some people will experience more silence and detachment, while others will experience more of the Shakti, the Cosmic Feminine Energy. There's no particular dogmatic road that it travels.

There certainly isn't "one God." There is a particular religion that invented that philosophy. I repeat, there is not "one God." In fact, there's no God, and only when you become humbled into such innocence to express that loving sentiment, does that which is referred to as God make itself known to you.

That Supreme Reality creates the atmosphere that it itself wants to live in, in you. That means it will never come to live in you as a limited and isolated spiritual identity. It will only live in itself—in and as you also. It will live in you, but only as it, without compromising any aspect of its immensity. So, it will only ultimately fit into itself. It will only realize itself. You will not realize it. How can you realize that which makes any form of realizing possible? How can that which is beyond knowledge itself be known? How can the immensity of the ocean be known, except to experience itself as both total ocean and as a drop? The drop contains the entire ocean in it. It has to look very carefully at its sub-structure. It has to look very minutely at its core. Then, it can say, "I am Oceanic. I am Vast. I am the Vastness itself," without going to any so-called ocean, without even moving from where it is.

The general problem is that people want to make a deal

with God in a fear-based state. They think that, first of all, God is other and separate and that life is an ethical affair, that life is a moral affair. Life is completely amoral and has not an ounce of ethics in it. Life is just the excruciating play of energies, period. And you happen to have been brought into this for no discernable reason, for no reason that you will ever discern.

You are the mystery and when the mystery stops trying to figure things out, the Mystery comes. When you stop begging to your fictitious deity for redemption, salvation, and forgiveness, when you give up the whole sordid affair of selfishly wanting something for yourself, then that which you are answers to itself. Then, the echo of your longing appears clearly and unmistakably, rings like a bell, and that bell rings into Silence.

*There's Only You, December 24, 2005, DVD #17*

# If Coming into This Room Means Anything, It Means That You've Finally Let Loose into Yourself

The mind is a perfect tool for action, to guide action, to incept action, to complete action. It's a marvelous measuring device, very much like the lens of a camera. It helps you hone in, focus, clarify, and then produce a bright and clear image of what you wish to capture.

But the mind can never measure the immeasurable Feeling of Being. No matter how much it tries to adjust its focusing lens onto that Immeasurable Consciousness, it will always find it foggy, vague, mysterious, elusive, subtle, transcendental. My message is really not to guide your mind to a particular area, but to have your own head descend into your Heart.

I'm not afraid to pause and to feel the space that's always in unison with you. For me, the sole aim is not to make sense in a purely discursive and rational way. I'm much more interested in something else, something that is neither within you, nor within me—something that is outstretched between us, beyond us, and also exists as us. It's not that it's not us, but it's more than us. It's us and something immeasurable.

Coming into the awareness of this is what I call meditation. This meditation is love. It's relating. It's not just talking about what feels immeasurable, but it's actually firing out that Immeasurable Consciousness as intensity. The word I like to use is Shakti, which means, force or power of Consciousness. It's important to know that it's not some kind of external force, some kind of relative power. It's the power of Being itself, which is effulgent, radiant—it's Bliss.

Once you become deeply vulnerable to this Feeling of Being, you can begin to awaken into it immediately, even if you're a spiritual novice, even if you don't have any sadhana behind you, that is, even if you haven't really done spiritual practices. There's such a quickening of Intoxicated-Love-Energy that manifests here that you could come right into it.

Attentiveness, with love in your heart, is the best way to approach it. I don't want to use the word concentration. Concentration, to me, is a shrinking down of attention. I'd rather use the phrase: "full of attentive caringness" or "full of attentive concern." If you have that, and you're really listening, and you really care to listen, you'll spontaneously be ushered out of your subjectivity—that is, your relative subjectivity, which is composed of thought, feeling, sensation. It's not that we deny those things. We fulfill them. They begin to attach themselves to that Radiance, which is beyond all of them, and they begin to dissolve their personal identity, their personal function. They go beyond functionality into this Feeling of Wholeness, of Love.

Don't be surprised that having come here with a certain intention, you become spontaneously weaned of that. You may have something that's really gripping you from the inside. It's defining you. In a way, it's constricting you. But something magical begins to happen, in spite of that, without you even having to erase that. It goes away. You become more enamored of something else. You become more fascinated.

You must have this kind of flight of fancy about yourself, if you want to arrive at the highest levels of Consciousness. You can't be overly practical. You shouldn't be a "space-cadet" either. You shouldn't be so other-worldly and dreamy that you don't have any affection for practical life. There's no merit in that. You can still perform action in the world, while being in that enamored state of Devotional Transcendence.

By dwelling upon That, you become realized in That. That begins to open you. It begins to draw you in. It begins to make love to you. You'll start to feel ecstatic, and I don't mean that in any limited way. You'll become profoundly ecstatic; not all the time, but you'll have such an ascension into that Immeasurable Consciousness that you become inundated with it—and then you may become a radiator of it. That's the most important thing; you begin to radiate spontaneously this Heart Awakened State.

What's happening is that you are meditating most reverently on me, on my words. But I'm also meditating most reverently upon you, upon the way in which your attention is functioning now. It's Reciprocally Radiant Reverence. In essence, that is Devotion.

Take a breath. Relax right into where you are. Let yourself be easy. The Transmission is here. It's active. There's nothing to hold you back. If coming into this room means anything, it means that you've finally let loose into yourself. You can explore, you can descend, you can transcend, ascend. You can be where you are spiritually. It's rare to go into a place where you can be yourself spiritually, that is, where you'll be met on your own terrain, on your own spiritual terrain, within your own level of present realization, and then begin to spontaneously join in an ascending movement of Consciousness and Energy.

Most religious pursuits are exoterical, conventional. They're extravagant social clubs. This is actually the esoteric quintessence of Realization itself. This is going beyond all kinds of relative pursuits to know and understand and it's a gift. It's just a gift that happens here. It's a spontaneously arising gesture.

*Reverence, Ecstasy, Benediction, May 6, 2004, DVD #8*

## Every Particle in Your Being Becomes Like a Radiant Flame of Attention

My own mind has been utterly deconstructed into simplicity. I'm not even in a position to package something and then give it to you. I'm wondering if you see the implication of that, where that puts me. I am not even allowed to separate one iota from what I am doing from what I am about to do.

The Realized State is not anti-intellectual. It is not anti-mental, but there's a great sense of radiance that the mind functions in, that allows it to function differently. There's a sense of being released beyond suffering, beyond conceptualization. That sense of suffering-less-ness is utterly liberal. It has a great, broad sense of compassionate liberalness built into it, which means it's not uptight. It's immensely relaxed about everything. It has no moral imperative, no moral directive. It's not out to be good. It's beyond the notion of good, and therefore, it's beyond the notion of not good, and therefore it's beyond relativity. It functions in this freedom of true innocence, total innocence, which is the Heart of the human being. It's not a created sense of innocence. It's not even the kind of innocence that you imagine that a baby has. It's a radically different kind of innocence.

Just listen with your whole body now. Listen with the ears

that are within the ears. See with the eyes that are within your eyes. Know with the Heart that is within your heart. You'll see I'm not talking to you. I'm just breathing, emoting in that simple state of innocence, without cause or direction.

You can feel the Energetic Thrill of this present moment, which is not a moment. You can feel the movement of thrilling energy in this moment, projected from some unknown location—not projected from a location to somewhere else. Rather, this is the Self-Generated Energy of Being, self-manifesting, spontaneously revealing the presence of Light, Feeling, and Energy.

Once you realize this, you become this. You don't worry about what's after death. You don't care what's after death. There is no "after death." That's a sick creation of the mechanistic mind. You don't even know what's ahead of you five minutes from now, a half hour from now. That's the way death is going to be. Death is an idea.

It's not necessary to stay in the waking state right now. It's okay to let yourself go. I'm not talking to you personally anyway, so to speak, so let yourself go. Whatever sensation there is now, give yourself to it; just give yourself, give into it. For once, give in.

Don't hold yourself up in superior isolation, superior separation. You may have to do that when you function, because you function in a binary system of opposites where one thing has to beat down the other thing for something to get done, but in this space we're not doing that.

This isn't the victory of one opposite over another or the speaker over the audience. It's where we all become mindlessly hollow, where we become hollowed out and therefore transparent and free.

Just Energy is talking now, just living, Vibrant Energy is talking and it's speaking just to give a context to this being-together. It has no ulterior motive.

Are you in me? Are we all submerged in that same Non-Localized Feeling? Do we feel submerged in that Radiated Intensity, that intensity that is Radiance?

This thing cannot be packaged, can't be sold, can't be purchased, and thus, let yourself go. Do not hold onto the waking state. There is nothing there. This is a place where you can become dysfunctional, disassembled, deconstructed, released from yourself. So, go into that, don't hold back.

Every religious scripture has tried to point to this state, this magnificent, super-abundant sense of Being. Every religion has tried to name it, wrap it in its rituals, suffocate it with its philosophy, its theology. And every one has systematically and utterly failed. In order to approach it, they've tried separating good from evil. They've tried separating spirit from world, inner from outer, sacred from profane, love from non-love and it's all failed. Every devious approach to it has failed and thus its triumph, which it takes no credit for, which it makes no claim upon.

You know, it's all about being able to bear this Bliss of Being and Consciousness, to live in that unbearableness of Being, to just live in it and allow it to live in you. Can you allow yourself to come apart enough to reside in a state of Absolute Beatitude, without any guilt? At some point, because you've allowed yourself over time to exist in that dismantled state, everything in you catches fire, every particle of your being becomes like a Radiant Flame of Attention, something that cannot be put to use. It's there just to burn bright. That flame will spontaneously kindle itself over and over again.

You become the Light of the world, the Light of the Self. You become the field of Non-Duality. You are the field of Non-Duality, at the same time the field of Radiant Energy, at the same time the field of Feeling or Love—all three.

So, you could never, at any point, say it's this lineage or it comes from this tradition. It doesn't come from anything. It never came from anything. You can't put it in any box. It didn't come from any box and you can't put it back in any box.

When you burn through that final worldly convention, which is the whole language of salvation, liberation, enlightenment, when you burn through that, then you are That. Only That can burn through that final hypnotic trance, that spell of duality—only Consciousness itself, surviving in its own Intensity will keep itself perfectly free from all of that gibberish, all of those rumors, riddles, all of those silly things they talk about.

You finally grow up and you're not really of this world at all. So, if you communicate at that point, it will be in the spirit of poetry, music. It will be pointing to a whole different dimension.

We are in That presently.

*Organic Functioning, December 14, 2004, DVD #18*

The only way to end suffering is to plunge into the silence of the Self, into that place where suffering has already been conquered. You can spend eons trying to unravel the knot of your own misery, deconstructing various fears and limitations, yet never awaken permanently—for any form of deliberate action will only strengthen the knot of separation. Even successful spiritual practices will tend to create subtler and subtler aspects of "the me." Enlightenment therefore, only arrives in the form of a Gift. After all efforts have failed, locate Grace and surrender to That, whether in the form of a living Spiritual Master or within the Invisible Absolute of your own Self. Grace is the Master, whether He speaks or remains silent.

part [7]

Grace

# This Is Not a "Nothing to Do" Teaching

I rely on the native power within Being and not any kind of yoga that I've mastered, any kind of spiritual approach, any kind of teaching. It's not because I don't value approaches or I look down upon them. They are just not appropriate for what I do.

I rely on the Transmission-Power of my own life to create the teaching. I depend completely on that. Everything I am, everything I teach, comes from a place that's beyond me.

It simply mysteriously shows up through what you might call Grace, which means, for no reason at all. That's how I define Grace, something happening for no reason at all. Grace is not some positive wind from the beyond blowing into relativity. It's not some positive breath of God. Grace is that anything happens at all. So this happens of its own accord. What happens around me, and through me, and beyond me, happens through Grace.

Most seekers are looking for a new security blanket to put on them, to feel good in life. "Give me a new set of beliefs. Give me some new approaches. Give me a new set of techniques. Give me some new ideas. Give me Self-inquiry." Give me this and give me that.

I want to take everything from you. This is in a whole different category. I'm not going to give you the Self. The Self isn't yours to take. The Self is not an object, nor is it an escape hatch for the personality to indulge.

There is a difference in approaching what's called realization as some kind of goal to be attained, as opposed to just sitting here and literally emptying out with me, and just being taken over by Consciousness. Do you see the difference?

The Buddhists are obsessed with accruing merit. They don't ask what good all this merit is going to be in the end and what this thing is that is accumulating it. And if you ask those questions you would have to deconstruct all of Buddhism. So, this is about the absence of attainment.

Not that you just become lazy and stupid because David says there's "nothing to do." This is not a "nothing to do" teaching. It may require that you do an awful lot of meditation. I just don't know. I leave that up to you to find out. I'm just not going to take on that very dualistic relationship with you.

*Approach Me Naturally, March 5, 2010, DVD #30*


# All the Faith You Harness Will Be from Your Own Experience

This is the Creative Power of the universe that's being offered to you as sadhana, as Waking-Up-Power. It's just a question of time. It's like the sun shining on a piece of ice. It just depends on how thick the ice is and how hot that sun can get.

If we have an inner relationship, that's perfect. If you know that we are together on the inside, that Consciousness is meeting you in this context, that's all you need. You can't be fooled because it's all about you recognizing this.

I don't make any effort to convince people that things are happening. But once you start recognizing what's happening, that's a whole different story. So, if you don't need to be talked into this, and your own realization summons up this kind of description, then it's being done. Your transmutation into Consciousness is happening.

And this is unbelievable. The word unbelievable is a good word, because you really can't wrap your mind around this. This is about unwrapping and unraveling the mind itself and opening it to the Source-Consciousness.

All the faith that you harness will be through your own experience. The deep faith and trust and perseverance you've shown in continuing to come here, entering into this relationship, is based on your own Self-Recognition. It's the natural outcome of the truth having been revealed to you.

So, I'm not in the business of promising things to people. I don't say, "well if you come here this is going to happen." I wait for you to speak up and let me know what's happening. Then, I'll say something like: "yes that sounds right." That way you're always fully dependent on yourself. You're not dependent on me. Otherwise, it's not real. If it's not you, it's not real.

*Seeing Consciousness, February 3, 2010, DVD # 29*

# The Movement of Divine Energy

It sounds reductionistic to say that there's nothing on the inside and nothing on the outside. So, what's the whole point? Just to be here, just to look through these eyes, to experience this nervous system, to be alive, that's the point.

Human beings invent meaning. They invent stories to describe what the ultimate meaning may be. But we all know that they're just stories, great mythological stories, sometimes great archetypal stories, which deliver the intellect into the field of the imagination.

And in that imaginative consciousness, there's a full appreciation of the nature of poetry, metaphor, drama, all co-existing within Consciousness. So, imagination is not a pejorative term. In fact, it's an exalted one.

The Grace, the movement of Divine Energy in space and time, to look and listen out of one's entire being, to simply know, is the hallmark of a purified life, a purified consciousness, and a purified nervous system.

*The Field of Feeling, July 2, 2002, DVD #7*

# Enlightenment Is the Tacit Realization That You Are God, You Are Consciousness

Enlightenment is the tacit realization that you are God, you are Consciousness, you are the universe, the entirety of it, not just a piece, and then all that follows from that.

If you're the entirety, then you begin to take on global concerns in your life. Everything is thought about in enormous perspectives. In other words, you become the world and you take responsibility for it directly, in that way, energetically, meaning your energy is running everything. It means your functioning is this whole world, in motion. When you have that kind of lucid awareness, it changes the whole field of your action, not just the content of it, but the flavor of it, the depth of it, the fabric of it, so that the whole becomes seeable in you. You reverberate the whole. You reverberate in the whole, the wholeness of existence.

Therefore, you are no longer just an individual body-mind, walking and talking, dancing and playing. You still continue all that, but with the radical shift at the very base of your being that you are Consciousness, and therefore everything proceeds out of you. This whole world proceeds out of you, in you and out of you. You are the first and the last, the alpha and the omega.

In that state of awareness, you are spontaneously nourishing to all things. Everything draws nourishment from the emanation of your Radiance. You become extremely aware of symbiosis, how everything is living off everything else. Everything is in a position of giving over everything it is to everything else. That is the dance of life, that everything is drawing and giving. Once this opening has occurred, sufficiently, that will be your realization, not just some pretty concept.

And there's no love possible without this radical shift. Love is not just a fancy thought, just a sweet idea in the mind. Love contains the ferocious energy of organic processes. It contains both the beauty and the devastation that you see in nature. Ripening in maturity, inner maturity, psychological maturity, metaphysical maturity, spiritual maturity are the pre-conditions for launching out on this voyage.

You could never convince someone intellectually to be reborn spiritually. For something so profound happens in this awakening that it can be likened to the birth process. It's that shocking, that graphic a transformation. It's that visceral. It's like being born.

When you're dealing with something so profound and so serious as the transformation of life into Cosmic Reality, then only the inborn grace of hunger can provoke and maintain that. And there's no challenge that's accepted within this invitation, unless there is the simultaneous realization that there are no guarantees.

This is not about getting a warranty from the universe, claiming that you were perfect at birth and you're destined to realize it in this new, transformative process that you've begun. There's no guarantee. And that's what makes it particularly ferocious and real and also non-replicable. You don't get another chance, even if you believe in reincarnation. After all, it's just energy that's reincarnated, if it in fact occurs.

*Into the Beyond, March 18, 2006, DVD #21*

# That Anyone Could Come into Full Awakening and Then Go on Living, That's an Indescribable Benediction

The most auspicious thing to do is to find a spiritual practice that connects you with your own Life-Energy, your own Consciousness, and practice that. That's the best way to approach enlightenment, because you'll never get to enlightenment by reading about it. It's not in a book. It's not in a series of books. It's something that comes about through these interrupted periods in your life when there is an influx of spontaneous grace. It's when you're thrown off track, when you start to meet the unpredictable, that you get this glimpse of That which is beyond time.

It's a miracle that you could come into this and live it. That's what I'm getting at. That anyone could come into full awakening and then go on living, that's an indescribable benediction. That you even have achieved full awakening is almost impossible. It's so rare to come into That alone. If that happens, something magnificent has happened. But, if you come into it so deeply that you move in That, you talk in That, you do everything that you do in that Supreme Consciousness, that's a profound miracle, that's something that there's no category for.

One hasn't lost one's discrimination. One hasn't suffered the loss of one's devotion. Both are fully intact. The capacity to love is intact and the capacity to transcend everything is intact.

What is it that allows for this kind of flowering to happen? It's an atmosphere of trust and innocence. That is what an awakened atmosphere is—a trusting, innocent atmosphere where nothing is imposed on the individual.

This realization comes from within each one of us. It's not something that comes from me to you or from some mysterious source to you. It's a flowering of life from within itself. Nothing can come between That and you—no text, nothing.

Here, the silence is just as important as the words. If there's a long lapse of silence, it means that there's something more profound occurring than speech.

*Shiva and Shakti, June 3, 2003, DVD #18*

# You've Got to Find That Part of You That's Fiery and Insatiable and Wants to Taste The Nectar of the Absolute

I like to say that there are three different Transmissions that are active. There's Divine Light, which is "advaitic." It's the essence of non-separation, non-separative awareness. Secondly, there is Divine Love, which is this enormous welling up of feeling, of gratitude and/or energy in the heart area. It comes from realizing exactly where you are; exactly what's being offered. There's a kind of exhilaration and exuberance in knowing that, in feeling the Light. There's a spontaneous, immediate reaction of appreciation and then, beyond that, there's just this raw, Primal Energy of communicated Bliss, as meditation itself, as Kundalini-Shakti.

These three things are all active simultaneously. So, no matter what obstacles you have, say goodbye to them.

It's joy! I'm firmly convinced of this. Even though there's evidence everywhere I look to not believe this, I only believe this. I don't merely believe it, for belief is so shallow and superficial. I am utterly convinced of it. It has convinced me from my own experiences and through what is beyond experience that That is always present and available.

Is it possible to be in such a high state of awakeness and still be a human being? Yes. You still have faults. I would say it's more important to become unified with the source of all action, to become stationed there in your awareness, than it is for you to perform so-called virtuous action. I would say that there's a virtue in being established in Consciousness, which transcends all kinds of temporary virtues and attainments.

Not that you shouldn't do relative acts of virtue. I'm not saying don't do them. But I'm saying that when you connect back into your Consciousness, with clarity and depth, there's no greater force of benediction on this planet, on any planet (if you believe in other planets, other worlds).

There's an aspect of you, which is beyond every world, this gross world and the subtlest states of thought and perception. There's something in you, which is immeasurably beneficent, beyond all manifestation, beyond being even confined to any particular form of meditation, manifestation. This is Grace. This is the awareness of Grace, that the Transcendental Consciousness, the Pure Consciousness, the One Reality, the One Divine Reality is the most important core of everything. But, this is something you have to realize. It's not something you can believe.

You've got to find that part of you that's fiery and insatiable and wants to dine on the Absolute Consciousness, that wants to taste the nectar of the Absolute. It's that fervor that destroys your obstacles. That's Kali, that's the Destructress, that love for Life, for Consciousness, for Awakening. That love will manifest its own weapons, so to speak, to destroy anything that's holding you back. So, the key is just focus on accentuating your love of Consciousness, your love of your own Transcendental Self.

You can do it through dance. You can do it through formal meditation. You may do it through an art form. There are many ways to travel this path. Sometimes you won't do it through anything. You'll just do it internally, without associating it with any activity.

Right in this moment, you can actually feel the Fire of Reality burning. This is associating with that which is truth, not my truth, not your truth—no one's ownership.

Can you relax and just be Consciousness itself? Can you relax and just feel Consciousness manifesting in you, as you? For that to happen, many of your vasanas have to be uprooted, burnt away.

*Reverence, Ecstasy, Benediction, May 6, 2004, DVD #8*

# I Want This for You a Trillion Times More than You Want It for Yourself

*Participant:* Is there anything in the context of a spiritual practice, outside of meditation, that can assist in the eradication of the doer?

*David:* No, not if it's a strategy, not the way you're asking. Who's going to do it?

Let me. I'm doing that. This is what this meeting is. Don't worry about anything. I want to give this to you much more than you want it for yourself. I want this for you a trillion times more than you want it for yourself. You can't imagine. Why? Because I am that Self that's everywhere, wanting itself everywhere. It's that simple.

We build up a crust around our life through worldly functioning, through the marketplace, doing this and that. We have this encrustation happen, which covers our innocence. You need to uncover that. You need to taste your innocence again. Otherwise, you can't progress anywhere. You can't do anything right. Forget about eradicating "the me." Nothing will have meaning in your life, real significance, unless you taste the innocence of your being, the Love that you are, the Love that you don't need to find. That you can never become deserving of.

Eons will go by. You'll just keep torturing yourself. It's really hard. I know it's hard. I'm not minimizing your pain. I'm just telling you that there's no alternative for you but to hear me in this moment. There's really no alternative.

I have nothing that you don't have, except I struggled for many years to find this, like a madman. And you don't come out the way you think you're going to come out. You come out kind of maimed and in a strange way that will be known only to you. A part of you is profoundly wounded and stays in total woundedness, not "healedness." But, you're rent open. You're torn open. That Light gushes through. It's not necessarily going to polish every edge.

You see, you were imagining all this solid reality that never changes for you. That's what you were presuming. But that solid reality has a lot of holes in it and a lot of Light shining through it. Moment by moment, there's lots of transparency, no matter what state of consciousness you think you're in.

*Participant:* I came in today and as I meditated it was very painful for me. There was a lot of fear and body aches and wanting to run away and a lot of very uncomfortable stuff. And then the Transmission started to penetrate that and now the ease is beginning to enter. And the question I have is: it's all fine and good to feel the Bliss here. But then you walk out the door and it's gone.

*David:* For something to become the case always, first it has to come and go. You can call it commitment that keeps you glued to this whole process. But I would say it's something much deeper than will. There's a kind of desperate clinging to something, which you are not fully experiencing. But all of your being is gravitating toward this subject of awakening or enlightenment, liberation, whatever you want to call it.

And so for it to come and go is okay. It's the excruciating surrendering process you're describing, which is that you do come into this and then there is a release, even from the

Bliss back into what is very ordinary and perhaps painful, perhaps full of suffering or numbness. So, there are two things you have to do. One is to just keep repeating whatever produces the immersion of Bliss. Secondly, perform a practice of recollection and deconstruction of the notion that there is the same solid reality waiting for you out there. See through it all or stop resisting it all.

Whatever this feeling of separation is that distinguishes between what's happening in this room and what's happening when you get back to your ordinary life, know that this Condition exists beyond all of that and is free to come and go as it wishes. You must give it permission, like a wild dog on the street. You've got to give it permission to wander. It will never come to you through chasing it. The Self doesn't like to be approached. Bliss will respond negatively to the contraction to hold it. You know that.

And it's an unending kind of realization. No matter how many times you come into this Freedom and Joy and Bliss, there's a corresponding reaction from the relative personality. It re-knots itself. That's the excruciating movement of spiritual evolution. Nobody can escape that. But, it can be quickened.

That's where Grace comes in, the grace that my Self is your Self. If this can happen to me, it can happen to you. And really nothing has happened other than consciousness recognizing its own root in Being. I have realized nothing. I have realized just what you've realized. There's a bunch of chairs in here, a bunch of bodies. I see everything external. My body will want to eat in a few hours. I'm subject to all of the same things that you are. But this is always there, whether I'm doing one thing or the other, or not doing anything. And it doesn't matter. It doesn't free me even from my own personal suffering. You should know that.

It's just that something revolutionary has happened to the totality and I don't take it personally. I've learned the lesson. I've bitten my fingers too many times, thinking that it was for me.

That's why you're upset when you lose it. You have this presumption that there's a "me" in back of there, to receive it and to own it. It's very subtle. You know, it's infinitely subtle, infinitely tricky how the mind, no matter how much Bliss it gets, still comes back with great force, like a fist always there to greet you.

So just let me love you in this moment, this precious moment that we have. Let's be together and breathe together in the Supreme Consciousness of the universe. I just want to notice you. I'm eager. I love what you shared, actually. It was really beautiful, not beautiful in the sense of "pretty" beautiful, beautiful in the sense of ruthlessly honest. You're ruthlessly ready to share what's going on with you. You're not just accepting some word of hope from me and being deluded by it. You're already in the heart, yes?

*Participant:* During the meditation I had this intense longing. But I was allowing it. It was like a craving to allow it or the whole thing was craving. It was really painful and I just felt this heat, this huge amount of heat, and then I kind of took a vacation.

*David:* I'm more fascinated by the longing and the introduction of that great heat of desire. Culture teaches you to kill that. I teach you to resurrect it. So, me and culture, me and the world, are not friends. Human societies will treat you as a functional unit to be utilized for production. But I make you dysfunctionally God-Intoxicated. That's my role. So I am butting heads, always, with the establishments, with the religions, with the politicians, with anyone who wants to regimentize human life. I am the "anti-regimentizer." I am the revolutionary. I am the Fire.

*Receive This as a Gift, January 6, 2008, DVD #22*

# Grace Gifts Itself to You, through You, into You, and Then beyond You

The idea that you become totally free of fear is something of an exaggerated myth, trying to divorce the human element from enlightenment. So you get these very macho teachers saying, "I have no fear," and "I'm not afraid of death." You begin to form an image of them as supermen or superwomen, rather than as extremely vulnerable, tender human beings who also might have issues exactly as you do.

There is a quality of fearlessness. But that fearlessness has to do with being resolutely aware of who you are. It can even happen alongside some mild to moderate neuroses. I'm here to divest you and me of our superficial self-images and get to the core of reality, not to indulge in grandiose, super-spiritual imagery and metaphor. And this is very important in my teaching. You can be totally Divine and totally human at the same time. There's no problem. There's really no problem.

It's very important to get this impersonal level of intimacy with me. Whether you call it me or your higher Self, it doesn't matter. People who are inclined toward devotion speak of it as the teacher. People, who are inclined towards knowledge-based, or discrimination-based understanding, call it their own Self. It doesn't matter what you call it. It only matters that you have tasted this kind of freedom. As you can intuit, it's not to be possessed. It's a gift. The entire phenomenon of that sort of Grace comes as a wave, as a gift. It gifts itself over to you, into you, through you, and then beyond you.

You need to be humble. You can't get too filled with yourself, with all your knowledge of spiritual things and spiritual matters. This is all about non-knowing. It's very simple once you begin to grasp that your freedom is just beyond the edge of your mind. You learn to live there. You learn how to do it organismically. You don't need to be taught through techniques necessarily.

*Talks and Dialog on the Internet, Volume 5, July 24, 2009, DVD #I-5*

# It's the Liberating Power of Consciousness Itself That Enlightens—It's Not a Teaching

It's Consciousness that liberates. Consciousness is the Great Liberator. The Absolute is what frees you. Your own mind frees you only in so far as it is sinking, or rising, or cognizing that Absolute Reality. Then the mind is, or can be said to be, the bridge to realization, the path to awakening. Other than that, it has no real function other than to guide you in the field of action.

Later, when you become awakened, your action will become powerful, different. It will carry in back of it the impulse of Pure Reality, however you look in life. You can be on the street as a homeless person with dirty clothes and ripped socks and disheveled hair and still be carrying the force of Total Reality, while some well-bathed, well-dressed person in a three-piece suit is contributing to the demise of the whole world. So don't be fooled by appearances. Don't be fooled by words. Don't be fooled by images. Become keen to what's in back of the mind and then you can see out of your heart. You'll see everything directly.

Consciousness, when awakened, begins to radiate its own power and prowess of liberation. Do you understand? It's not about me teaching you anything. It's about awakening itself coming out full force, radiating itself, touching you in some way and letting it work on you. Therefore, it's the liberating power of Consciousness that enlightens. It's not a teaching. It's not a series of propositions. It's not a book you can read. It's not the activity of your own Self-inquiry or personal meditation. This is beyond all that.

Enjoy the Grace. All this is accomplished by the "siddhi" of my teaching, the" siddhi" of activated Consciousness, and the "siddhi" of your reception of it, all of which cannot be explained in human terms or physics-based concepts, at least not with Newtonian physics. This is something outside of the reach of time and space and yet it is occurring. Where? Right in time and space. It's time and space itself that leads beyond itself. You're being played already. You're in the dance already.

Consciousness is the Liberator. Awakened, released Consciouness flowing and flashing out of the Absolute spontaneously is the highest teaching. No teacher as a deliberate spectator or performer is necessary to teach that.

The Shakti within Consciousness is what I am refering to— its own potential for movement and Self-Transmission, the spontaneous transmission of itself.

These are all concepts about time and space. They're really about duality. But there's no other way we can talk, except from duality. If I talk completely from unity, it will just sound like a babbling brook or like the sound of a bird, which is what unity sounds like to somebody who's really listening.

If the world is still here, we'll be here next week and I look forward to that. But between now and then I'll forget all about it and just enjoy each moment. I hope you do the same. Namaste.

*Talks and Dialog on the Internet, Volume 3, December 2, 2008, DVD #I-3*

Grace is a gift given for no reason.

# Epilogue

Point Reyes National Seashore

# The Impact of Bliss

*Orley:* From a Participant in Peru: "Emotions like sadness, which come with identification with a certain story, are very difficult for me. I'd like to just rest from everything. Could you please talk about how to deal with them?"

*David:* See if you can let your emotions become attracted to this Bliss and have them attach to the Bliss. What I am talking about here is a simple displacement of the direction of the emotions and an appreciation for the all-pervasive Bliss that will arise in spite of any emotion.

At the same time, even though the Bliss arises independently of any emotional arising, it's still necessary for a human being to connect within his or her own attention. Connecting the Bliss within the emotional structure will result in a feeling of devotion, love and extreme happiness.

It's not possible to oppose the momentum of the emotions on their own level, especially when a human subject is feeling like a victim or controlled by certain emotions. Trying to wrestle the emotions apart from their attachments is very difficult.

But what is not so difficult is to engage your emotional nature toward this Bliss that we feel together. Let your emotions arise and be happy in that Bliss-Field. First the Bliss has to be detected. Once it is detected you might find a human happiness coming into the equation. So, it's not just impersonal Bliss, but it's also the happiness of the emotional structure in relationship to the arising Bliss. Let them fuse. Let them come together.

What you should not be concerned with is trying to dissolve your own story. You cannot take a negative approach toward realization: that is, one that is based on conflict, conflict between one part of your being and another.

So you have to dissolve that conflict by first understanding that there is nothing you can do, except put yourself in a position where Grace becomes available. The Grace, in the case of this teaching, will manifest as the impact of Bliss upon the body and mental structure. That will create release, release from the pattern, release from the story.

But the release from the story is never achieved on the basis of trying to end the story, or reacting to the story in any way. So put down this idea that you have to do something first in order to be free—just come as you are. Let yourself be naked here. You don't need to be in some modified state before you can enter into a relationship with me and with the Bliss itself.

Let's start right now. It's not possible for us to deal with what you recognize to be a pattern in your life. You cannot approach a pattern, an abstract pattern, which essentially is an interpretation and also a concept—a concept brought forward from the past into this moment.

So let's engage in an innocent play together in which the Shakti, Divine Light and Devotional Feeling can enter into your being right now. Then, if that happens, let me hear what you have to say at that point. I'd be interested to know whether and to what degree there is a transformation in what you perceive to be a problem right now.

*Orley:* The Participant responds, "I perceive a vibration in all my body and a silent peace."

*David:* Let me know when the peace becomes Bliss—if it does.

*Orley:* The Participant in Peru says, "I don't know if this is Bliss. Do you mean a physical sensation of Bliss?"

*David:* The physical could be included in the experience. But the word Bliss, translated from the Sanskrit word, Ananda, means fullness of happiness, satisfaction, inundation with a kind of spiritualized pleasure, happiness, contentment.

Bliss is a term to describe the fullness quality of the Absolute, not just the empty quality. When we talk about the empty quality of the Absolute, we mean its void-like nature, or its empty nature, empty of things, empty of experience. Therefore, that denotes a kind of negative aspect of the Absolute.

When I turn you toward Bliss and the recognition of it, I am asking you to perceive the radiant quality of the Absolute—its shiny or glistening aspect, which creates, as it reflects into the brain, a kind of luminosity.

It also saturates the heart in satisfaction, contentment, happiness, joy, fullness, overflowing fullness of satisfaction. It means all those things. It means more than what I just pointed to. There's something even inexpressible about what Bliss is, except that it's a massive field of Satisfaction, Energy and Light.

*Orley:* From New York: "In the Webcast this morning, I felt huge gratitude. But I could not identify Bliss. Tonight I am blown away with Bliss and I actually feel that I can see radiant beauty in your form and feel that beauty in this moment so powerfully."

*David:* That's wonderful. Accept these gifts with great humility and love, and understand that a gift is a gift. A gift can never be possessed. It cannot be acquired. It cannot be lost. It can only be enjoyed, and for no reason other than it is what is real. It is what is the case, in this context of the Transmission of the Self. It is the transmission of Light, Energy and Feeling. Just keep coming into this and see what develops inside of you, of your whole being. Just keep on engaging this to no end, to no foreseeable end, without looking for any particular result, not being prejudiced in any way like that, staying innocent, open, full of generosity, and so on.

*Orley:* From Peru: "I feel everything is okay, like nothing can disturb this Being-ness and sadness is welcome here. It's not here anymore, actually."

*David:* That's a very keen recognition. It's good that you're looking in this way and that you can describe your experience so simply and so accurately.

As I was saying to the previous viewer, who made such a beautiful comment, let's engage this in a way where we feel free from the desire to end this connection. In other words, try not to see this as a simple step in a direction you are taking in your life. But instead let this step be the only step.

Don't use me as a means to an end. Become everything with me. Become everything in me. If you have that attitude, you will revoke the linear, goal-directed mind and embrace more generous spirit. You will release the grasping that causes limitation and disappointment and you will begin to enter into a different kind of experience, one that goes on and on. This requires continual recognition, the continual help of Grace, the reception of Spiritual Current, or Spiritual Radiance, and a willingness to work through and to abide with whatever comes up—to let everything go and therefore to return back into this Bliss-Field, this Bliss-Condition, which is just the nature of Self.

*Orley:* The Participant from Peru comments, "Now I know I can merge sadness into the peace."

*David:* Don't say, "I can." Just say that sadness merges into peace. We can get rid of the I-factor and accept it as a gift, as a non-attainment. When you have very deep spiritual experiences and you don't attach to the attainment aspect of it, you get the best result, you get the most powerful effect. In this way, there is nothing for the "me." There is nothing for the "me" to grasp or hold, possess or own. The "me" will be seen through naturally, effortlessly, and if it's not seen through it will become identified with Bliss. So don't worry about the seeing-through language. Don't get caught there. All the language I use is just a tool. It's just there to help you release into this Openness. Then, the miraculous powers of Being will convince you of the rest, of whatever you need to see, whatever you need to understand.

The key is to let it happen spontaneously, without contracting. If contraction happens, then that's just part of what arises, as "what is"—in "what is"—so it's just to be noticed and then it will be bypassed naturally without any specific kind of strategy to ameliorate it. So just relax and be easy.

215

Don't worry about anything. Nothing can hold back this Bliss. You can imagine something called ignorance and make an argument that it prevents Bliss from coming through, realization from coming through, but that's just mind-stuff. That's just intellectual argument.

The truth is that the ground of Being as it arises in experience has more potency, more dissolving power, more activating power, than any other phenomenon. So, it's its own teaching. It's not subordinate to anything else. It's not subordinate to psychology or psychological theories. It's not subordinate to religion and theological theories.

The Self, as pure Being, is what realizes. There's only one Self. There's only one Being. It's not out there, nor is it in here. It's an omnipresent Field. It's in all directions. It has no particular beginning or ending. It's Pure Recognition. It's Pure Understanding. It's Pure Feeling. It's Pure Knowing. There's nothing outside of it.

That's the call to understanding and also the call to taste it—both are necessary.

Continue a gentle meditation schedule at home. Put some space aside, some time aside, to perform sacred practices, practices which are done in a very loving way, to remember the Bliss that is always present. If you are having a difficult time due to the conditions of the world, or to the conditions of your subjectivity, then put some time aside in your daily life, on a daily basis, to enjoy a continuation of what we do here together.

You can still come back here even after you construct your own schedule, your own practice. Whatever you construct should be simple and basic and in tune with your intuitive nature, which means it grasps, it inherently grasps, the way awakening happens spontaneously, and it simply cultures that. It further cultures that phenomenon—just what you experience here, you could say.

*A Live Webcast Talk, September 17, 2014*

## Grace

Grace is the Ultimate Reality. In the Vedic tradition, it is said that the Self is the Ultimate Reality. Being beyond experience, it's difficult to know what is meant by the Self. It remains an unknown, a mysterious idea or concept that posits an unknowable reality—one that is ever present: undying, unborn, always eternally itself, never losing itself in the process of change. The more we say about it, the less there is to be understood.

Grace offers another way to formulate what this Ultimate Reality is in terms of human experience. Since human experience, specifically, is lacking in the *understanding* of the Self, one can utilize the term grace in what I feel is a much better idea or concept. The way I use the word grace is that something simply happens. Whether you look at the birth of a human being or the birth of a solar system, the birth of plant life, animal life, the birth of weather patterns, you will not be able to see a completely strung out series of causes and effects that completely explain that event or those events. Through scientific thinking you can, by analyzing certain intimate cause and effect relationships, make statements about what causes what. But that's through a kind of microcosmic analysis of things, using induction and deduction, the two forms of reasoning.

Yet when we are dealing with a whole universe and when we are dealing with our movements in space and time, in our body-minds, moment by moment, we can't use science to ask what is the reason for that, what gives rise to that. Science can offer no specific explanation. So it's deficient in that understanding, which perceives relations among objects. It specializes in describing perceivable, perceptible, measurable relationships among objects. From those measurements and perceptions, it then makes postulations, theories, assertions. But what it does not afford is an ultimate understanding of Reality. The reason for that may be that there is none.

That is why I suggest the use of the word grace, which is that something happens rather than nothing. That something happens, that this world is, is simply Grace, which doesn't really explain anything. Yet it says enough for the mind, or perhaps the intuition, to enjoy a sense of restfulness inside of the mind about the appearance of everything.

Grace is a gift given for no reason. It's that something occurs rather than not occurs. You can't imagine a non-occurrence. That's a negative event. It's also a contradiction in terms, because if it didn't occur you wouldn't even know that it didn't occur. A non-occurrence is a concept analogous to nothingness. It really has no meaning, since even saying nothingness posits a kind of something—that's how we imagine it. That's how we imagine the meanings of words, the meaning of every word. And you cannot create a word that describes total lack and there may be a good reason for that, which is that there is only Being. There is only Substance. There is no lack of substance, no lack of being in ourselves, in the world, in the universe.

It may seem when certain aspects of appearance are taken away from us, such as when someone dies, or when we lose something, that there is a minus. But as time goes on that minus turns itself into a kind of forgetfulness. That minus is not a positive minus. It's not an actual accrual of loss. Rather, it is the simple loss of a memory.

Grace operates inside of both areas where there is no substantial reality, in terms of explaining why existence is, and at the same time it offers a kind of affluence to the one who contemplates the nature of Grace.

It cannot be denied that we are, that this is. Existence is, life is, the body is, and no matter how much reductionistic analysis we do with science or any other body of knowledge or technique to know, we never can answer adequately with the answers that we receive, the truth, the final truth.

Things come and go. Things arise and pass away. That paradox, in the midst of what seems to be an abiding fullness, the positivity I was speaking of earlier in terms of everything being Being and not non-being, seems to tie the mind up in such a way that it can only end up in a kind of wonder. Coming into being and passing away is a sufficient contradiction to wrestle us from an anxiety-based approach to knowing.

Science is an anxiety-based approach to knowing, unless you're dealing with certain areas of science, which are purely theoretical, which don't engage in any practical application, but which are geared toward thought learning how to think itself. In other words, science which moves towards metaphysics and philosophy. That sort of scientific understanding will be more in the direction of spirituality—not religion—spirituality, which is metaphysics. Things coming into being and passing away can never make sense as a final perception about the nature of things.

Grace arrives in sufficient time to meet that paradox or contradiction, since it does not attempt to confront the contradiction directly, nor does it sidestep away from the contradiction of change. Grace represents a whole new thrust in human consciousness, the acknowledgment of it, the appreciation of it. That it is not "an it" is part of its wonder. Grace simply seems to say nothing. Its power is in its quick arrival in a Field, which is obvious, but unable to be approached.

Grace rescues us from the pitfalls of knowing, of believing that we have to know. At the same time it does not affirm a faith-based understanding. Faith is an aggressive assault against the unknown. Like science, it's an anxiety-based response. Faith is an intimidating force against the easiness of not-knowing. Faith is faithless. It's bad faith, as Jean Paul Sartre once wrote. It's bad faith, not affirmative faith, not positive faith. It's a lack of any genuine appreciation of Grace. Faith is grace-less, as religion is grace-less. It's un-graced in its forceful and willful character against that which we cannot know.

Grace, finally, is the liberating potency of Life itself to give Luminescence, to give Knowledge, to Enlighten the knower, not about anything, but just to rest in the inherent and simple lucidity in the Light of Existence. So we never have to leave existence to be graced. We never have to not be present. We never have to go somewhere else, either in the mind or with the body.

Grace is that something happens, anything that happens: a planet, a smile, a good meal. The good meal is not something that is the cause and effect outcome of everything that happened before. Action has this quality of mystical unknowingness about its result, and that is what I am pointing to with Grace: everything being action, everything is Grace.

You can analyze piecemeal movements in existence, as science does, but you actually attain nothing of the actual fragrance of what is a moving existence, an existence which is movement, where its own movements are not kept track of in order to drive forward into the future to offer a finished result.

Bliss is the Feeling of Grace in the Heart. It arises for no reason. It is itself Realization. It's the signal of Realization. It's the mysterious Light of Being permeated in the Self, in the Bliss of the Self, and because of that, something called the Heart flowers, something which is Grace, which is Bliss, which is Light, shines from inside of itself. It's a Light that is not lit by anything else.

*A Live Webcast Talk, November 25, 2015*

**2011**-Point Reyes National Seashore

# Author Biography

David began his spiritual path or sadhana at the age of seventeen.

The first part of David's sadhana was the reception of an East Indian meditation initiation. As a result of this initiation, he soon began having many extraordinary spiritual experiences, both in and out of meditation.

In 1989, David embarked upon a second phase of sadhana. From approximately 1989–1997 he formed spiritual connections with two individuals known to be Avatars.

In 1998, David gave his first spiritual teachings in Santa Fe, New Mexico.

Subsequently he moved to Southern California, and taught there for several years before moving to his current location in Northern California.

Presently, in addition to Public Programs, David offers Live Webcasts, which draw in participants from all over the world. These Webcasts are an invitation to enjoy David's Transmission of Divine Light, Devotional Love, and Kundalini-Shakti.

Visit davidspero.org for more information.

Everybody's on this path. They may call it different things, but there's only one path, and that's to go from you to You. It's become so complicated.

I'm not a leader. I am not a spiritual leader and I am not a religious authority. I'm here as a spiritual friend to facilitate, to offer, to be as I am with you as you are. You don't need to change anything about yourself.